ME AND THE WORLD

First published in the United States of America in 2020 by Chronicle Books LLC.
Originally published in Spanish in 2019 under the title *Yo y el mundo* by Zahorí Books.

Library of Congress Cataloging-in-Publication Data available.

ISBN 978-1-4521-7887-5

Manufactured in China.

Text by Mireia Trius.
Illustrations by Joana Casals.
Design by Joana Casals and Mariam Quraishi.
English translation by Feather Flores.
Typeset in Gotham.
The illustrations in this book were rendered digitally.

10 9 8 7 6 5 4 3 2 1

Chronicle Books LLC
680 Second Street
San Francisco, California 94107

Chronicle Books—we see things differently.
Become part of our community at www.chroniclekids.com.

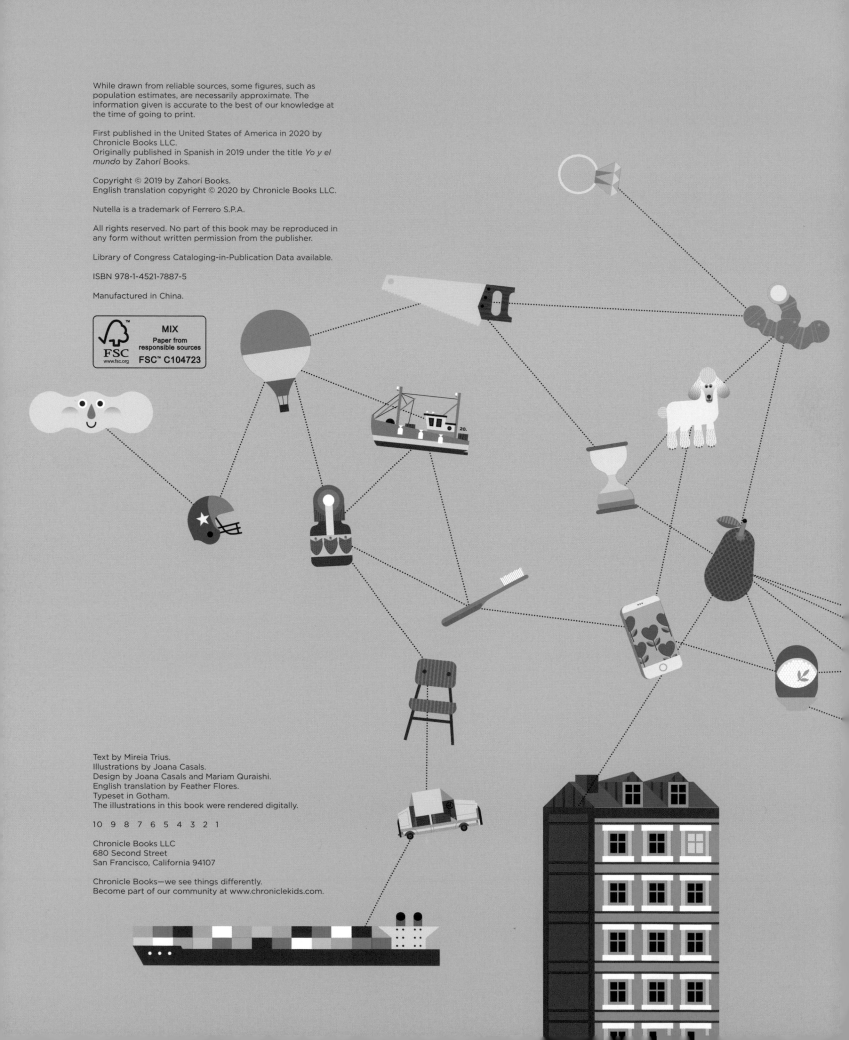

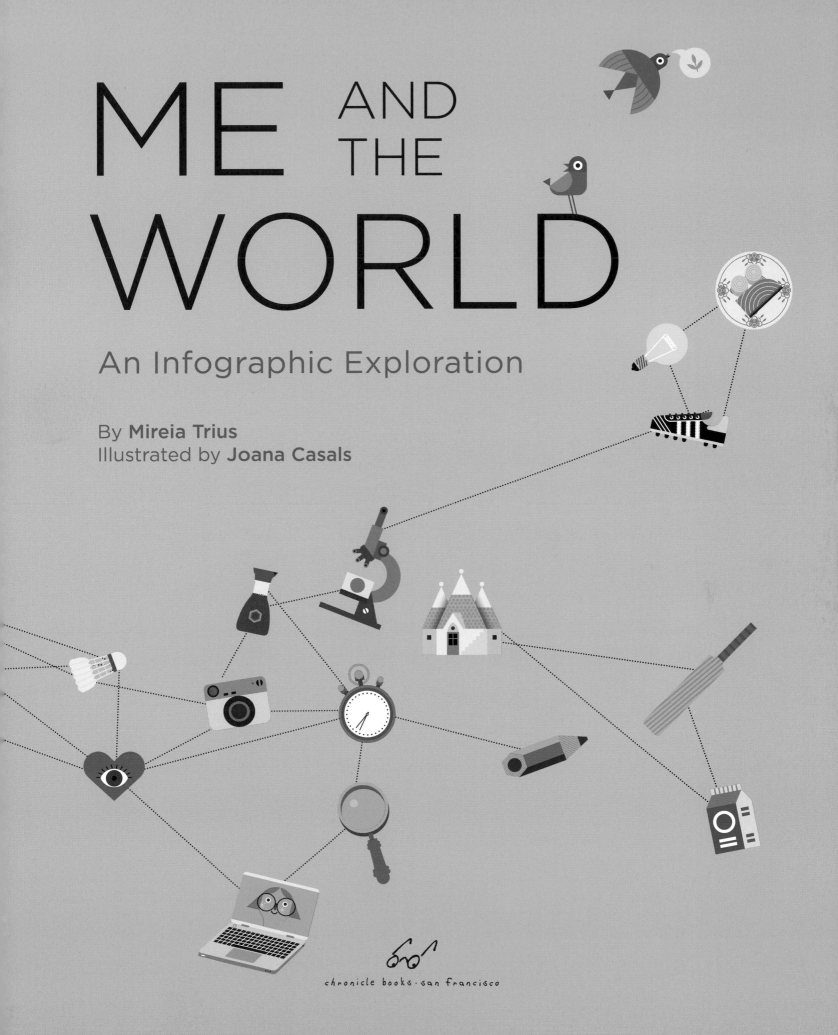

ME AND THE WORLD

An Infographic Exploration

By **Mireia Trius**
Illustrated by **Joana Casals**

chronicle books · san francisco

TABLE OF CONTENTS

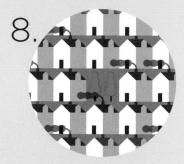

Inuk
Ivaana

Aron
Helka

Liam
Olivia

Lucas
Em

Emily
Oliver
Olivia
Lucas
William
Ida
Jack
Julia
Paul
Marie
Gabriel
Emma
Liam
Emma

João
Maria
Hugo
Marc
Martina
Lucia
Mul
Mo

Mohamed
Salima

Mohamed
Yasmine

Mamadou
Fatamata

This is my country

Santiago
Sofia

Sebastián
Camila

Santiago
Luciana

Luis
María

Miguel
Alice

Ramón
María

Mateo
Augustina

Juan
Julieta

Santiago
Sofia

Most common or highly common names of children around the world, in recent years

1. COMMON NAMES

MY NAME IS LUCIA, AND I'M FROM SPAIN. MY BROTHER'S NAME IS HUGO. OUR NAMES ARE
COMMON WHERE I COME FROM, BUT EACH COUNTRY HAS ITS OWN POPULAR NAMES.

2. TYPES OF FAMILIES

I HAVE ONE BROTHER, AND HE IS YOUNGER THAN ME. MY PARENTS HAVE LOTS OF BROTHERS AND SISTERS, BUT TODAY IN MOST PARTS OF THE WORLD IT IS MORE COMMON FOR FAMILIES TO HAVE THREE KIDS OR FEWER. THERE ARE SO MANY DIFFERENT TYPES OF FAMILIES, MORE THAN WE CAN EVEN COUNT HERE! WHAT KIND OF FAMILY DO YOU HAVE?

1/ AVERAGE HOUSEHOLD SIZE AROUND THE WORLD

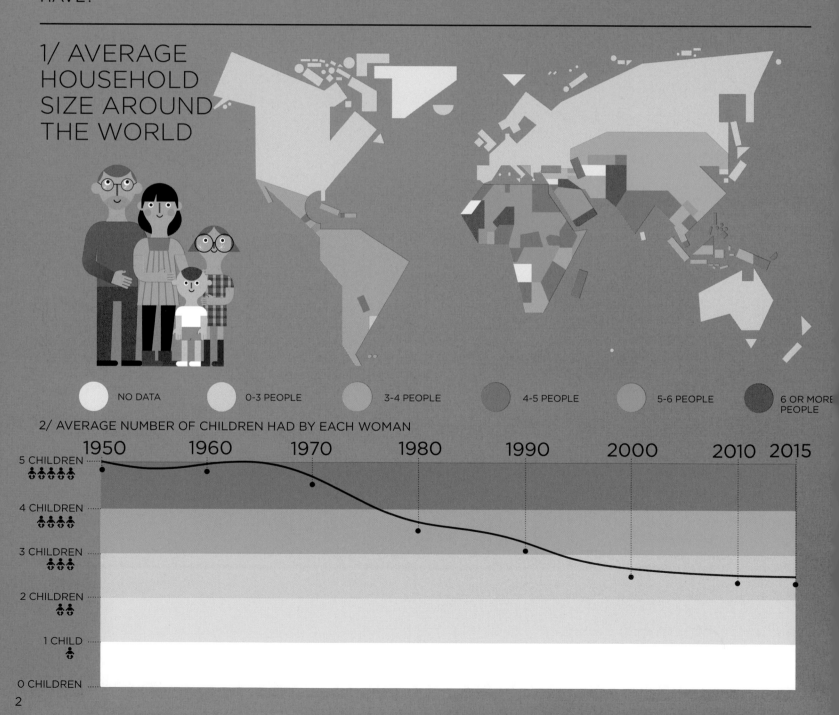

NO DATA   0-3 PEOPLE   3-4 PEOPLE   4-5 PEOPLE   5-6 PEOPLE   6 OR MORE PEOPLE

2/ AVERAGE NUMBER OF CHILDREN HAD BY EACH WOMAN

1950   1960   1970   1980   1990   2000   2010 2015

5 CHILDREN

4 CHILDREN

3 CHILDREN

2 CHILDREN

1 CHILD

0 CHILDREN

3/ DIFFERENT FAMILY STRUCTURES
BASED ON DATA COLLECTED FROM FAMILIES IN THE UNITED STATES

1 adult + 1 child

1 grandparent
+ 1 child

2 adults
+ 1 child

This is my family

1 adult
+ 2 children

2 grandparents
+ 1 child

2 adults
+ 1 child

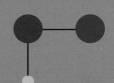

1 adult
+ 1 child
+ 1 grandparent

1 adult
+ 1 child
+ 1 other family member

2 adults
+ 2 children

2 adults
+ 1 child
+ 1 child

1 adult
+ 3 children

2 adults
+ 2 children

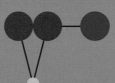

2 adults
+ 1 child
+ 1 grandparent

2 grandparents
+ 1 adult
+ 1 child

1 grandparent
+ 1 adult
+ 2 children

2 adults
+ 1 child
+ 1 other family member

1 adult
+ 1 child

2 adults

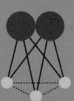

2 adults
+ 1 child
+ 1 child

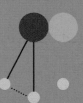

2 adults
+ 3 children

2 adults
+ 3 children

1 adult
+ 1 other family member

1 adult
+ 1 child

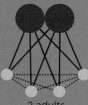

2 adults
+ 2 children
+ 1 grandparent

2 adults
+ 1 child
+ 2 grandparents

2 adults
+ 2 children
+ 1 other family member

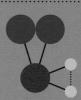

2 grandparents
+ 1 adult
+ 2 children

2 adults
+ 1 child
+ 1 child
+ 1 child

2 adults
+ 4 children

2 adults
+ 2 children
+ 2 grandparents

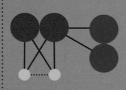

2 adults
+ 2 children
+ 2 children

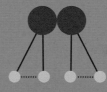

2 grandparents
+ 2 children

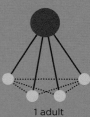

1 adult
+ 4 children

Family members:

Child   **Parent, care-giver, or other adult**   **Grandparent**   **Extended or other family member**

Relationships:

Partners or married   **Biological parent or child**   **Siblings or half siblings**

3. PETS

MY OTHER FAMILY MEMBER IS OUR BEAGLE, VITO. MANY FAMILIES HAVE PETS, BUT DOGS ARE THE MOST POPULAR PET OF ALL. SOME DOG BREEDS ARE WELL-KNOWN AROUND THE ENTIRE WORLD!

1/ TEN MOST POPULAR DOGS IN THE WORLD

1 LABRADOR RETRIEVER

2 GERMAN SHEPHERD

3 POODLE (ALL SIZES)

4 CHIHUAHUA

5 GOLDEN RETRIEVER

This is my dog, Vito!

2/ FAMILIES WITH PETS

57%
Have pets

43%
Don't have pets

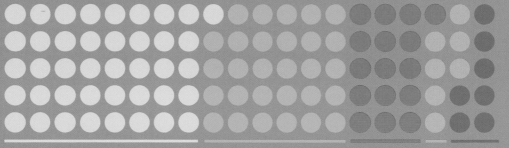

DOGS CATS

BIRDS FISH

OTHER

| 41.25% | 28.75% | 15% | 7.5% | 7.5% |

4/ MOST POPULAR PETS BY COUNTRY
BASED ON DATA COLLECTED FROM 22 COUNTRIES, IN WHICH MULTIPLE ANSWERS WERE POSSIBLE

CHINA	FRANCE	GERMANY	ITALY	JAPAN	POLAND	RUSSIA	SOUTH KOREA	SPAIN	TURKEY	UNITED KINGDOM	UNITED STATES
25%	29%	21%	39%	17%	45%	29%	20%	37%	12%	27%	50%
10%	41%	29%	34%	14%	32%	57%	6%	23%	15%	27%	39%
17%	12%	9%	11%	9%	12%	11%	7%	9%	16%	9%	11%
5%	5%	6%	8%	2%	7%	9%	1%	11%	20%	4%	6%

6
YORKSHIRE TERRIER

7
DACHSHUND (ALL SIZES)

8
BEAGLE

9
BOXER

10
MINIATURE SCHNAUZER

4. WORLD POPULATION

SPAIN IS ONE OF THE LARGEST COUNTRIES IN EUROPE, BUT IT ISN'T ONE OF THE LARGEST IN THE ENTIRE WORLD. IT HAS A POPULATION OF 46 MILLION PEOPLE. THAT MAY SEEM LIKE A LOT OF PEOPLE, BUT COMPARED TO THE POPULATIONS OF COUNTRIES LIKE CHINA OR INDIA, IT'S JUST A SMALL BALL ON THE MAP OF THE WORLD.

1/ COUNTRIES ACCORDING TO THEIR NUMBER OF INHABITANTS

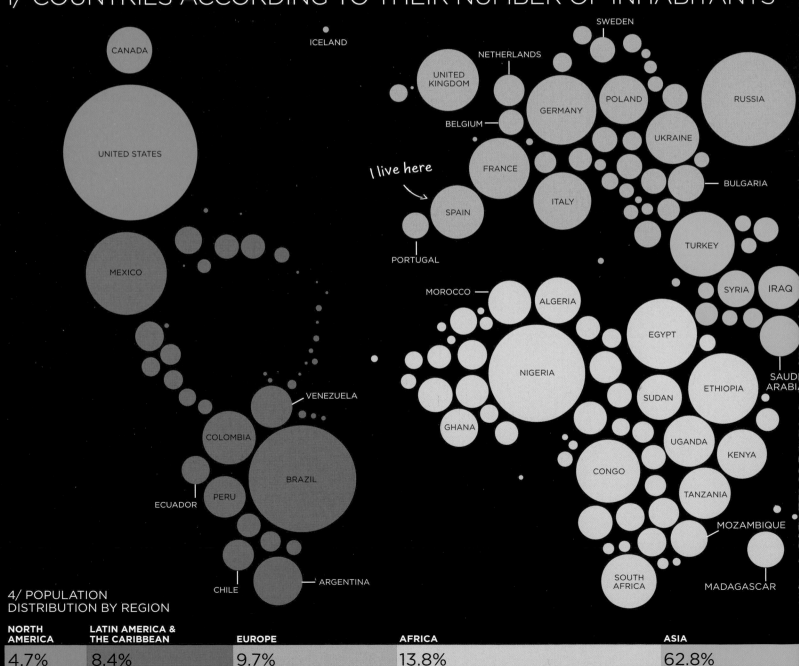

ICELAND
CANADA
SWEDEN
NETHERLANDS
UNITED KINGDOM
POLAND
RUSSIA
UNITED STATES
GERMANY
BELGIUM
UKRAINE
I live here
FRANCE
BULGARIA
ITALY
SPAIN
TURKEY
PORTUGAL
MEXICO
MOROCCO
ALGERIA
SYRIA
IRAQ
EGYPT
SAUDI ARABIA
NIGERIA
ETHIOPIA
SUDAN
VENEZUELA
GHANA
COLOMBIA
UGANDA
KENYA
CONGO
BRAZIL
TANZANIA
PERU
ECUADOR
MOZAMBIQUE
SOUTH AFRICA
MADAGASCAR
CHILE
ARGENTINA

4/ POPULATION DISTRIBUTION BY REGION

NORTH AMERICA	LATIN AMERICA & THE CARIBBEAN	EUROPE	AFRICA	ASIA
4.7%	8.4%	9.7%	13.8%	62.8%

2/ PERCENTAGE OF WOMEN AND MEN IN THE WORLD
BASED ON DATA RECOGNIZING ONLY TWO GENDER OPTIONS

WOMEN
49.55%

MEN
50.45%

3/ PROJECTED POPULATION IN FUTURE DECADES
BASED ON AVERAGES FROM A PROJECTED POPULATION RANGE

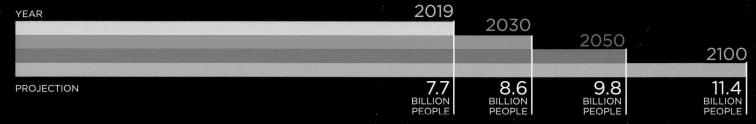

YEAR

2019
2030
2050
2100

PROJECTION

7.7 BILLION PEOPLE
8.6 BILLION PEOPLE
9.8 BILLION PEOPLE
11.4 BILLION PEOPLE

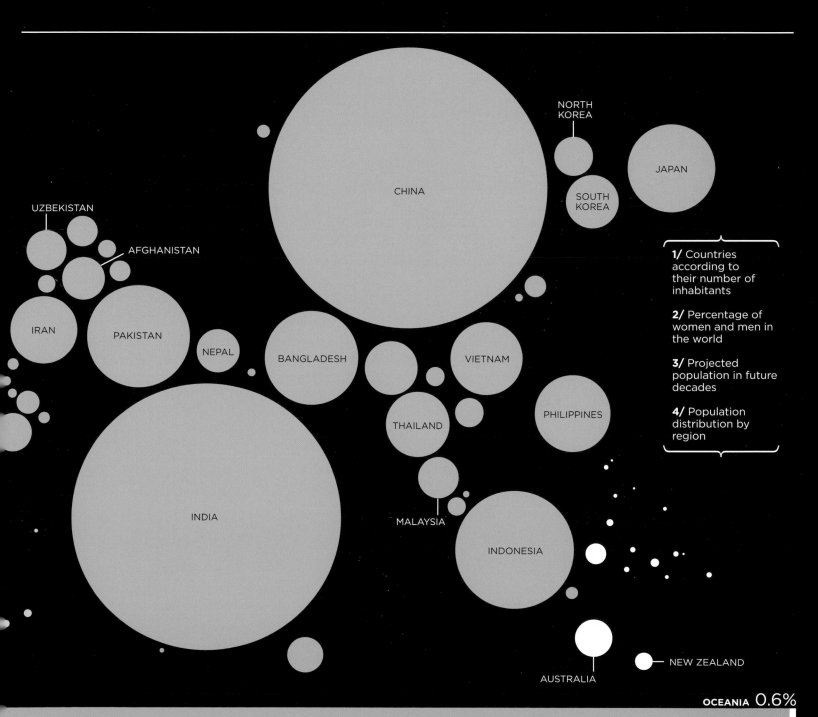

NORTH KOREA

JAPAN

CHINA

SOUTH KOREA

UZBEKISTAN

AFGHANISTAN

IRAN

PAKISTAN

NEPAL

BANGLADESH

VIETNAM

1/ Countries according to their number of inhabitants

2/ Percentage of women and men in the world

3/ Projected population in future decades

4/ Population distribution by region

THAILAND

PHILIPPINES

INDIA

MALAYSIA

INDONESIA

NEW ZEALAND

AUSTRALIA

OCEANIA 0.6%

1/ MOST WIDELY SPOKEN LANGUAGES IN THE WORLD

This is my language

| 1 MILLION | CHINESE 1,311 | SPANISH 460 | ENGLISH 379 | HINDI 341 | ARABIC 319 | BENGALI 228 | PORTUGUESE 221 | RUSSIAN 154 | JAPANESE 128 | PUNJABI 119 |

5. LANGUAGES OF THE WORLD

AT HOME WE SPEAK SPANISH, AND AT SCHOOL WE LEARN ENGLISH. SPANISH IS A ROMANCE LANGUAGE DERIVED FROM LATIN, A COUSIN TO LANGUAGES LIKE FRENCH, ITALIAN, AND PORTUGUESE. SPANISH IS THE PRIMARY LANGUAGE SPOKEN IN MANY COUNTRIES. TODAY IT IS THE SECOND-MOST WIDELY SPOKEN LANGUAGE IN THE WORLD!

1-2/ Most widely spoken languages in the world

3/ Map of the most widely spoken languages in the world

4/ Languages most commonly studied as a second language

2/ MOST WIDELY SPOKEN LANGUAGES IN THE WORLD
SEVERAL CATEGORIES INCLUDE DIALECTS

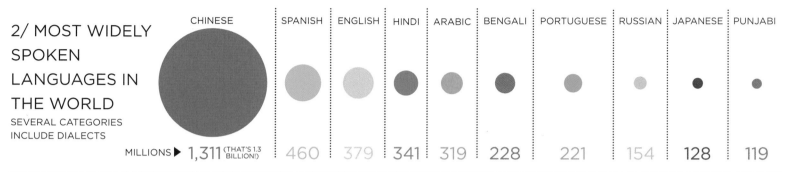

	CHINESE	SPANISH	ENGLISH	HINDI	ARABIC	BENGALI	PORTUGUESE	RUSSIAN	JAPANESE	PUNJABI
MILLIONS ▶	1,311 (THAT'S 1.3 BILLION!)	460	379	341	319	228	221	154	128	119

3/ MAP OF THE MOST WIDELY SPOKEN LANGUAGES IN THE WORLD

SPANISH · CHINESE · ENGLISH · RUSSIAN · PUNJABI · HINDI · PORTUGUESE · JAPANESE · ARABIC · FRENCH · BENGALI · OTHER OR MULTILINGUAL

4/ LANGUAGES MOST COMMONLY STUDIED AS A SECOND LANGUAGE

MILLIONS ▼

ENGLISH	1,500 (THAT'S 1.5 BILLION!)
FRENCH	82
CHINESE	30
SPANISH	14.5
GERMAN	14.5
ITALIAN	8
JAPANESE	3

6. JOBS AND PROFESSIONS

1/ SOME KINDS OF PROFESSIONS

1. COURIER / **2.** ORNITHOLOGIST / **3.** DENTIST / **4.** OPTOMETRIST / **5.** REFEREE / **6.** WATCHMAKER / **7.** PILOT / **8.** CAPTAIN / **9.** JEWELER / **10.** FISHMONGER / **11.** CARPENTER / **12.** MECHANIC / **13.** NURSE / **14.** VETERINARIAN / **15.** GEOLOGIST / **16.** WAITER / **17.** ASTRONAUT / **18.** TAILOR / **19.** MINER / **20.** FISHER / **21.** TEACHER / **22.** FIREFIGHTER / **23.** PHOTOGRAPHER / **24.** CYCLIST / **25.** COOK / **26.** ELECTRICIAN / **27.** HAIRDRESSER / **28.** DOCTOR / **29.** PAINTER / **30.** WRITER / **31.** MUSICIAN / **32.** BRICKLAYER / **33.** SCIENTIST / **34.** FLORIST / **35.** JUDGE / **36.** MAIL CARRIER / **37.** ARCHITECT / **38.** GARDENER / **39.** DETECTIVE

Dad's tool

Mom's patient

MY MOM IS A VETERINARIAN AND MY DAD IS A CARPENTER. THEIR PROFESSIONS HAVE BEEN AROUND FOR A LONG TIME, BUT THERE ARE NOW MORE JOBS RELATED TO THE INTERNET AND TECHNOLOGY THAN EVER BEFORE.

1/ Some kinds of professions

2/ Five jobs that didn't exist before 2005

3/ What do the more than 7 billion people in the world do?

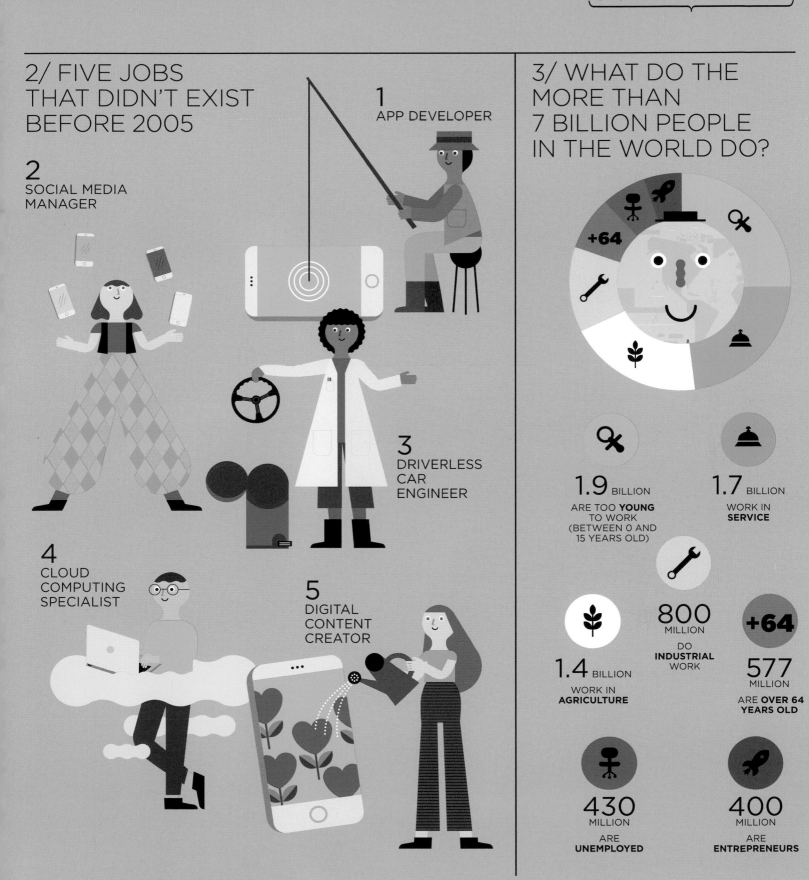

2/ FIVE JOBS THAT DIDN'T EXIST BEFORE 2005

2 SOCIAL MEDIA MANAGER

1 APP DEVELOPER

3 DRIVERLESS CAR ENGINEER

4 CLOUD COMPUTING SPECIALIST

5 DIGITAL CONTENT CREATOR

3/ WHAT DO THE MORE THAN 7 BILLION PEOPLE IN THE WORLD DO?

+64

1.9 BILLION ARE TOO **YOUNG** TO WORK (BETWEEN 0 AND 15 YEARS OLD)

1.7 BILLION WORK IN **SERVICE**

800 MILLION DO **INDUSTRIAL** WORK

1.4 BILLION WORK IN **AGRICULTURE**

+64 **577** MILLION ARE **OVER 64 YEARS OLD**

430 MILLION ARE **UNEMPLOYED**

400 MILLION ARE **ENTREPRENEURS**

11

1/ AVERAGE HOUSE SIZE IN DIFFERENT COUNTRIES

1/ Average house size in different countries

2/ Traditional houses from around the world

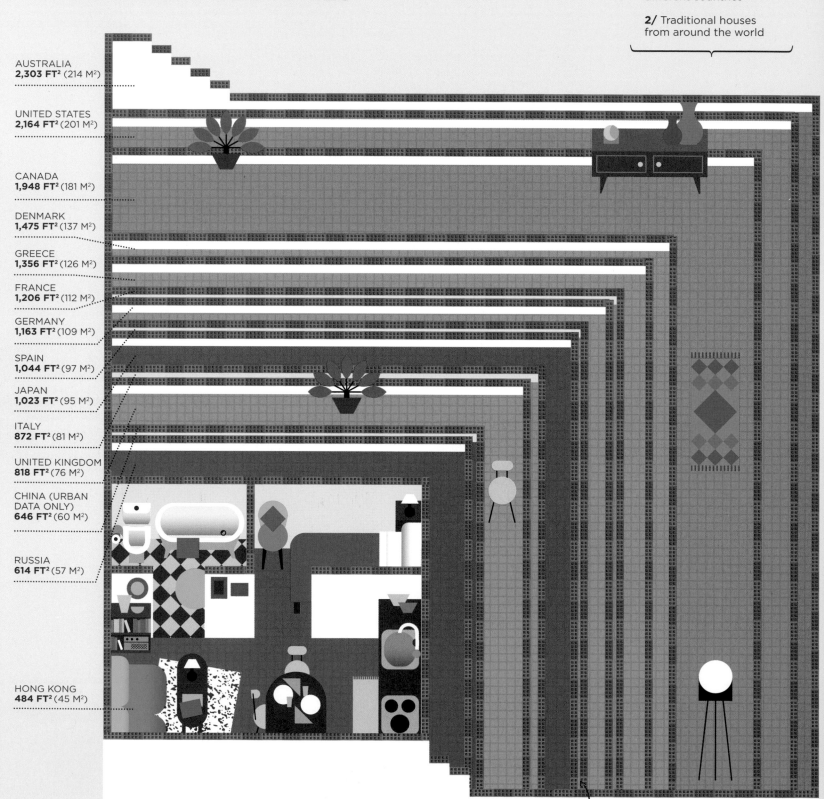

AUSTRALIA
2,303 FT² (214 M²)

UNITED STATES
2,164 FT² (201 M²)

CANADA
1,948 FT² (181 M²)

DENMARK
1,475 FT² (137 M²)

GREECE
1,356 FT² (126 M²)

FRANCE
1,206 FT² (112 M²)

GERMANY
1,163 FT² (109 M²)

SPAIN
1,044 FT² (97 M²)

JAPAN
1,023 FT² (95 M²)

ITALY
872 FT² (81 M²)

UNITED KINGDOM
818 FT² (76 M²)

CHINA (URBAN DATA ONLY)
646 FT² (60 M²)

RUSSIA
614 FT² (57 M²)

HONG KONG
484 FT² (45 M²)

This is the size of my house!

WE LIVE IN AN APARTMENT ON THE SECOND FLOOR OF A VERY TALL BUILDING. OUR APARTMENT IS NOT VERY BIG, BUT IT HAS LOTS OF SUNNY WINDOWS—AND WE CAN SEE THE OCEAN FROM OUR BALCONY! WE HAVE TWO BEDROOMS: ONE FOR MY PARENTS AND ANOTHER FOR MY BROTHER AND ME.

2/ TRADITIONAL HOUSES FROM AROUND THE WORLD

CHALET
ALPINE REGION

IZBA
RUSSIA

TRULLO
APULIA, ITALY

HALL HOUSE
UNITED KINGDOM

TURF HOUSE
ICELAND

RONDAVEL
SOUTH AFRICA

PALHEIRO
PORTUGAL

CONCH HOUSE
FLORIDA, UNITED STATES

IGLOO
CANADIAN ARCTIC

HANOK
KOREA

MINKA
JAPAN

MUDHIF
IRAQ

YURT
MONGOLIA

QUEENS-LANDER
AUSTRALIA

13

8. CITY POPULATIONS

I LIVE IN A CITY CALLED BARCELONA. IT IS NOT HUGE, BUT IT ISN'T SMALL EITHER. IT HAS ONE OF THE HIGHEST POPULATION DENSITIES IN EUROPE, WHICH MEANS THAT THERE ARE MANY PEOPLE LIVING IN THIS ONE AREA.

1/ SELECT URBAN AREAS BY NUMBER OF INHABITANTS

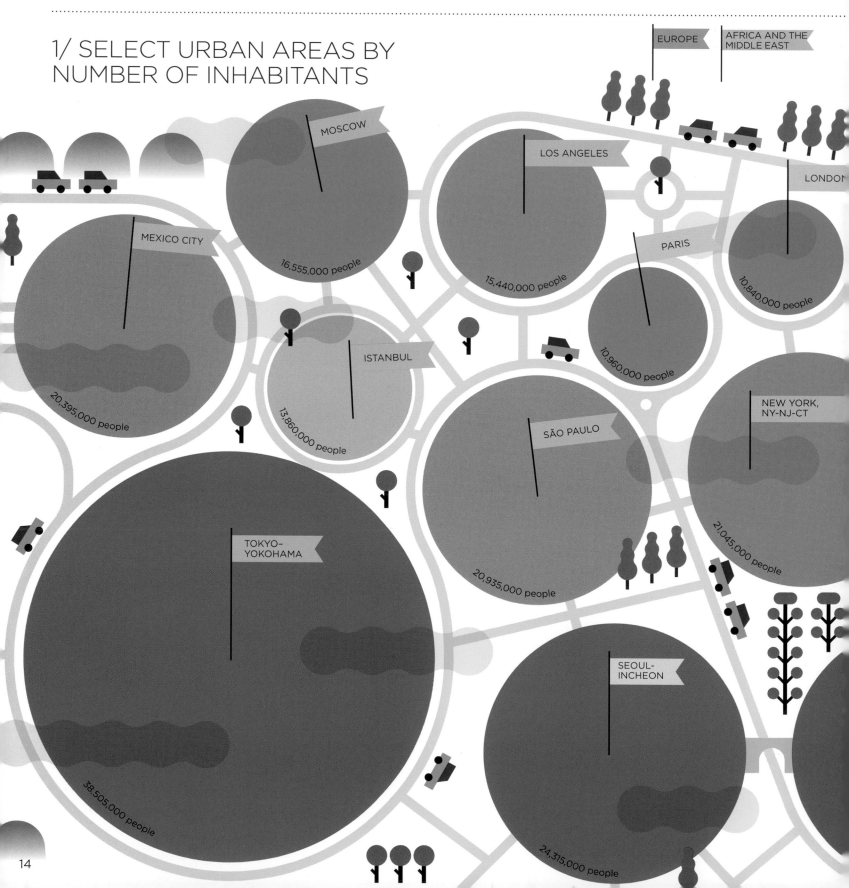

EUROPE

AFRICA AND THE MIDDLE EAST

MOSCOW
16,555,000 people

LOS ANGELES
15,440,000 people

LONDON
10,840,000 people

MEXICO CITY
20,395,000 people

PARIS
10,960,000 people

ISTANBUL
13,860,000 people

NEW YORK, NY-NJ-CT
21,045,000 people

SÃO PAULO
20,935,000 people

TOKYO-YOKOHAMA
38,505,000 people

SEOUL-INCHEON
24,315,000 people

1/ Select urban areas by number of inhabitants

2/ Select urban areas by population density

3/ Largest cities in 1950

4/ Largest cities predicted for 2030

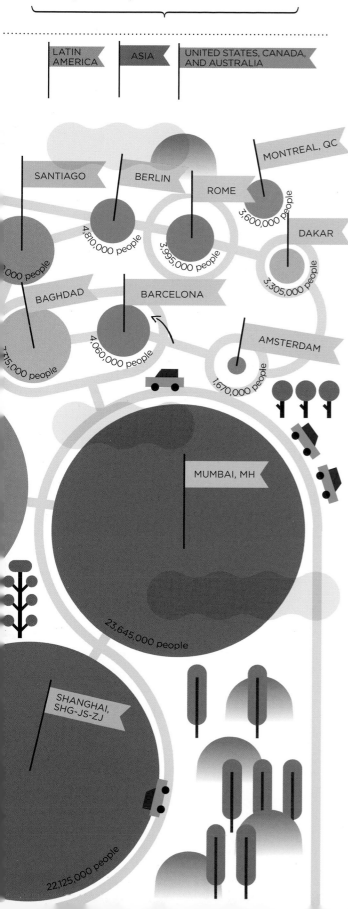

LATIN AMERICA

ASIA

UNITED STATES, CANADA, AND AUSTRALIA

MONTREAL, QC

SANTIAGO

BERLIN

ROME

3,600,000 people

DAKAR

4,810,000 people

3,995,000 people

3,305,000 people

BAGHDAD

BARCELONA

AMSTERDAM

4,060,000 people

1,670,000 people

MUMBAI, MH

23,645,000 people

SHANGHAI, SHG-JS-ZJ

22,125,000 people

2/ SELECT URBAN AREAS BY POPULATION DENSITY

FIGURES REPRESENT DATA IN SQUARE MILES

1 Mi^2 (2.6 Km^2)

1,000 PEOPLE

DHAKA
Bangladesh

MUMBAI
India

HONG KONG
China
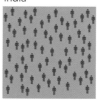

ALEXANDRIA
Egypt

ISTANBUL
Turkey

SEOUL- INCHEON
South Korea

MEXICO CITY
Mexico

GENOA
Italy
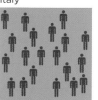

LONDON
United Kingdom

SANTIAGO
Chile

MADRID
Spain

MUNICH
Germany

PARIS
France
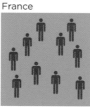

AMSTERDAM
The Netherlands
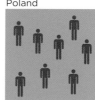

KATOWICE-
GLIWICE-TYCHY
Poland

NEW YORK,
NY-NJ-CT
United States

3/ LARGEST CITIES IN 1950

Millions

NEW YORK–NEWARK, United States — 12.4
TOKYO, Japan — 11.3
LONDON, United Kingdom — 8.4
OSAKA, Japan — 7.0
PARIS, France — 6.3
MOSCOW, Russia — 5.4
BUENOS AIRES, Argentina — 5.1
CHICAGO, United States — 5.0
KOLKATA, India — 4.5
SHANGHAI, China — 4.3

4/ LARGEST CITIES PREDICTED FOR 2030

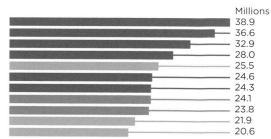

Millions

DELHI, India — 38.9
TOKYO, Japan — 36.6
SHANGHAI, China — 32.9
DHAKA, Bangladesh — 28.0
CAIRO, Egypt — 25.5
MUMBAI, India — 24.6
BEIJING, China — 24.3
MEXICO CITY, Mexico — 24.1
SÃO PAULO, Brazil — 23.8
KINSHASA, The Congo — 21.9
LAGOS, Nigeria — 20.6

9. BREAKFAST FOODS AROUND THE WORLD

JAPAN

◄ Miso soup, *tamagoyaki* (rolled omelet), a small piece of grilled salmon, and rice or *okayu* (rice porridge).

SPAIN

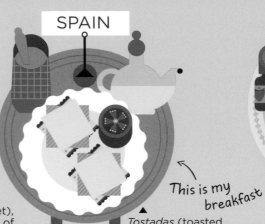

This is my breakfast

▲ *Tostadas* (toasted bread) with oil, cheese, ham, and tomatoes. A glass of hot chocolate.

TURKEY

▲ Bread, cheeses, butter, olives, eggs, tomatoes, cucumbers, jam, honey, and *kaymak* (clotted cream).

FRANCE

▲ Croissant or *tartine* (open-faced baguette) with butter and jam. A glass of orange juice or milk and a side of fruit.

ENGLAND

▲ Fried eggs, *bangers* (sausages), back bacon, cooked beans, mushrooms, tomatoes, and fried bread.

MALAWI

▲ *Phala* (cornmeal porridge), *chikondamoyo* (sweet corn cake), and boiled potato. A glass of hibiscus juice.

BRAZIL

▲ Bread with ham and/or cheese. *Bisnaguinha* (sweet bread) with *requeijão* (a soft, creamy cheese).

ICELAND

▲ *Hafragrautur* (warm oatmeal) with brown sugar, butter, maple syrup, and *súrmjólk* (a yogurt-like sour milk).

THE NETHERLANDS

▲ Slice of bread with butter and a thick coat of *hagelslag* (chocolate sprinkles). A glass of milk or *karnemelk* (buttermilk).

I USED TO THINK THAT KIDS ALL AROUND THE WORLD ATE THE SAME BREAKFAST AS ME. BUT THAT'S NOT TRUE AT ALL! IN KOREA, PEOPLE OFTEN START THEIR DAYS WITH SOUP; IN JAPAN, WITH SALMON; AND IN BRAZIL, SOMETIMES EVEN WITH COFFEE AND MILK!

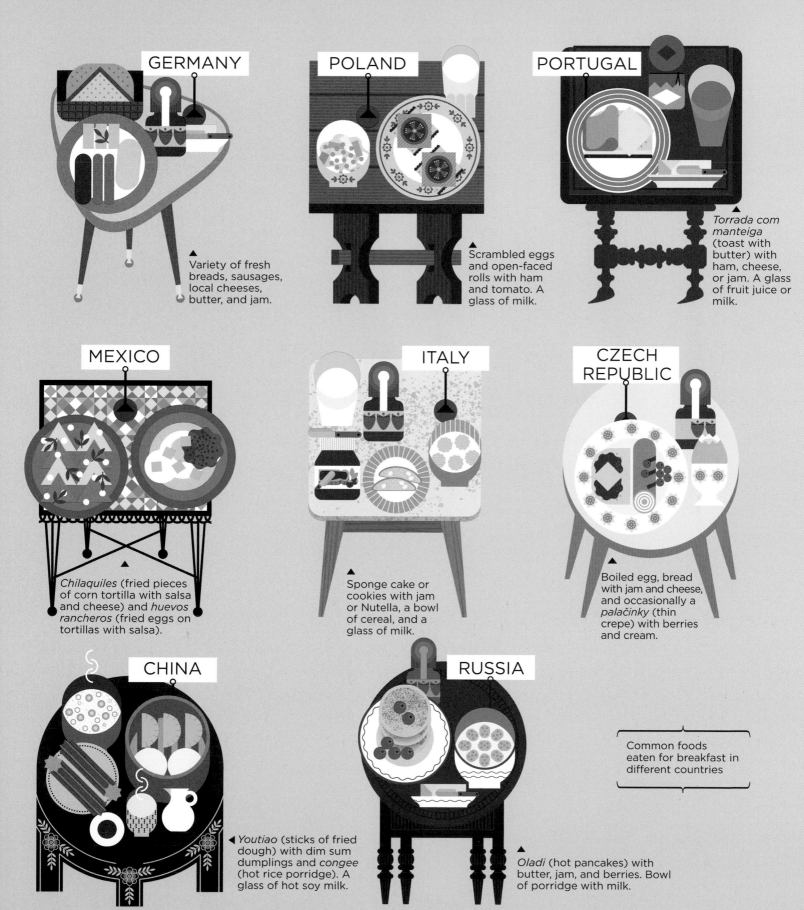

GERMANY

▲ Variety of fresh breads, sausages, local cheeses, butter, and jam.

POLAND

▲ Scrambled eggs and open-faced rolls with ham and tomato. A glass of milk.

PORTUGAL

▲ *Torrada com manteiga* (toast with butter) with ham, cheese, or jam. A glass of fruit juice or milk.

MEXICO

▲ *Chilaquiles* (fried pieces of corn tortilla with salsa and cheese) and *huevos rancheros* (fried eggs on tortillas with salsa).

ITALY

▲ Sponge cake or cookies with jam or Nutella, a bowl of cereal, and a glass of milk.

CZECH REPUBLIC

▲ Boiled egg, bread with jam and cheese, and occasionally a *palačinky* (thin crepe) with berries and cream.

CHINA

◄ *Youtiao* (sticks of fried dough) with dim sum dumplings and *congee* (hot rice porridge). A glass of hot soy milk.

RUSSIA

▲ *Oladi* (hot pancakes) with butter, jam, and berries. Bowl of porridge with milk.

Common foods eaten for breakfast in different countries

10. TRAFFIC IN THE CITY

1/ CITIES WITH THE MOST TRAFFIC IN THE WORLD
BASED ON NUMBER OF HOURS PER YEAR THAT THE AVERAGE COMMUTER SPENDS IN TRAFFIC

1 BOGOTÁ
Colombia

2 ROME
Italy

3 DUBLIN
Ireland

4 PARIS
France

5 ROSTOV-ON-DON
Russia

6 LONDON
United Kingdom

7 MILAN
Italy

8 BORDEAUX
France

9 MEXICO CITY
Mexico

10 MOSCOW
Russia

11 BELO HORIZONTE
Brazil

12 SAINT PETERSBURG
Russia

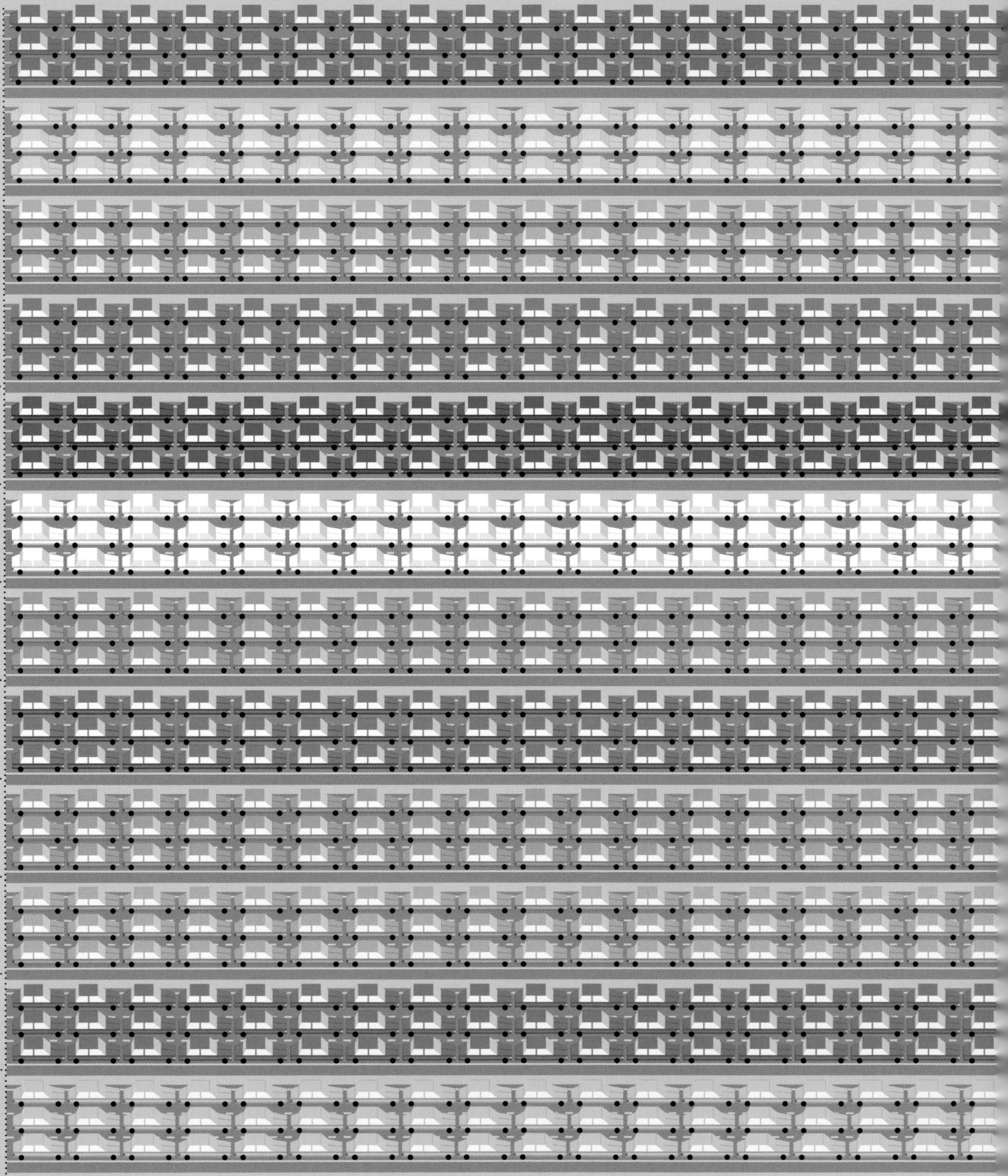

I LIVE CLOSE TO MY SCHOOL, AND THERE IS NOT A LOT OF TRAFFIC IN OUR CITY. IT ONLY TAKES US EIGHT MINUTES TO DRIVE FROM HOME TO SCHOOL. BUT THERE ARE SOME CITIES IN THE WORLD THAT HAVE SO MUCH TRAFFIC, IT CAN TAKE SOMEONE MORE THAN AN HOUR TO GET TO SCHOOL!

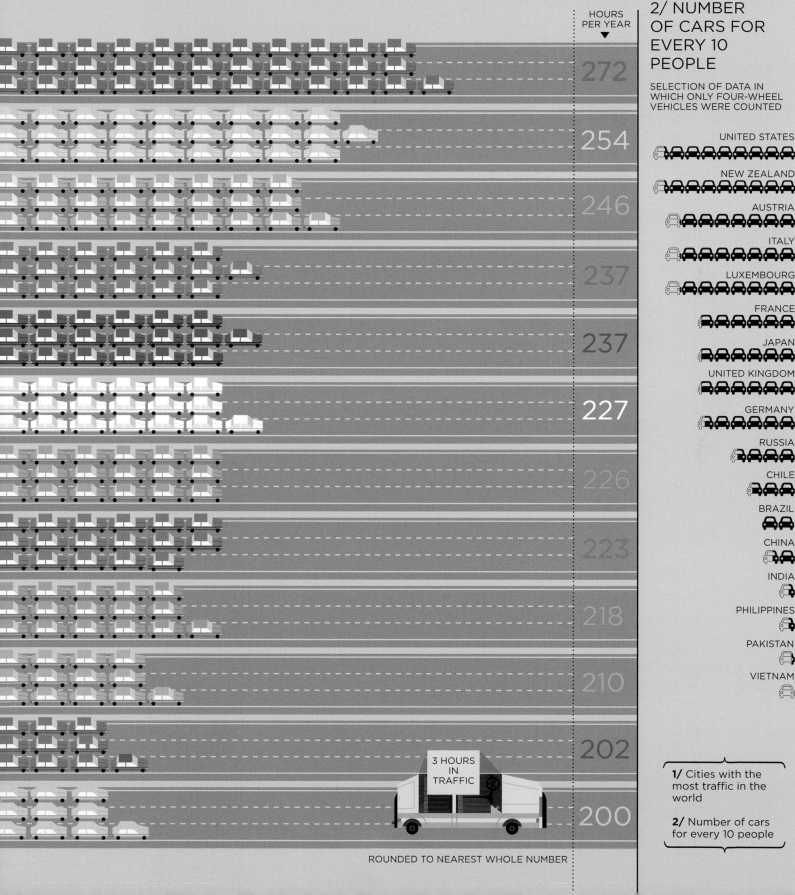

HOURS PER YEAR ▼

272
254
246
237
237
227
226
223
218
210
202
200

3 HOURS IN TRAFFIC

ROUNDED TO NEAREST WHOLE NUMBER

2/ NUMBER OF CARS FOR EVERY 10 PEOPLE

SELECTION OF DATA IN WHICH ONLY FOUR-WHEEL VEHICLES WERE COUNTED

UNITED STATES

NEW ZEALAND

AUSTRIA

ITALY

LUXEMBOURG

FRANCE

JAPAN

UNITED KINGDOM

GERMANY

RUSSIA

CHILE

BRAZIL

CHINA

INDIA

PHILIPPINES

PAKISTAN

VIETNAM

1/ Cities with the most traffic in the world

2/ Number of cars for every 10 people

19

11. AT SCHOOL

KIDS SPEND A LONG TIME IN SCHOOL, BUT NOT ALL SCHOOLS IN DIFFERENT COUNTRIES ARE ORGANIZED THE SAME WAY. IN SPAIN, OUR MANDATORY EDUCATION BEGINS AT 6 YEARS OLD AND ENDS AT 16 YEARS OLD.

THERE ARE STILL KIDS AROUND THE WORLD—MOST OF THEM GIRLS—WHO ARE NOT ABLE TO ATTEND SCHOOL, BUT FORTUNATELY THE NUMBER OF CHILDREN WHO DO GET TO ATTEND IS RISING OVER TIME.

1/ Hours and years spent in mandatory schooling

2-3/ Age at which children start school

4/ Number of children around the world who are not in school

5/ What are older students around the world studying?

1/ HOURS AND YEARS SPENT IN MANDATORY SCHOOLING
DATA IS REPRESENTED BY COLORED PENCIL BODIES, NOT DECORATIVE PENCIL TIPS

PRIMARY SCHOOL

SECONDARY SCHOOL

TOTAL NUMBER OF HOURS OF MANDATORY SCHOOLING

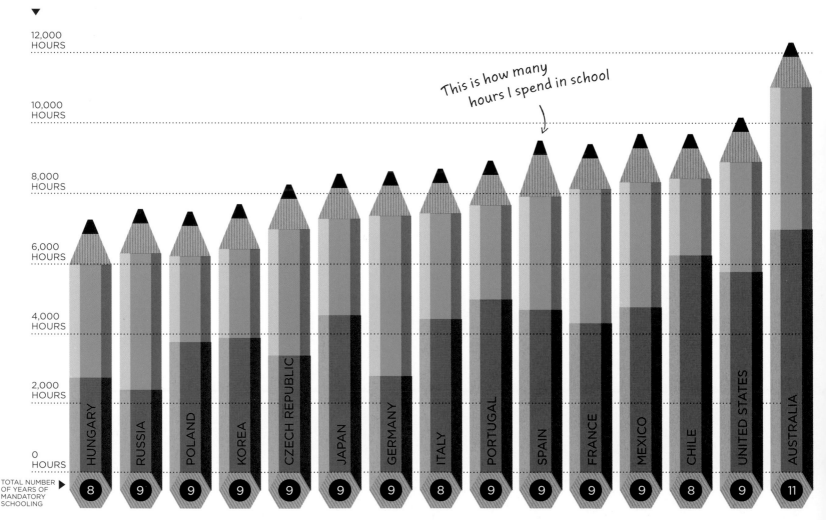

This is how many hours I spend in school

12,000 HOURS	
10,000 HOURS	
8,000 HOURS	
6,000 HOURS	
4,000 HOURS	
2,000 HOURS	
0 HOURS	

HUNGARY · RUSSIA · POLAND · KOREA · CZECH REPUBLIC · JAPAN · GERMANY · ITALY · PORTUGAL · SPAIN · FRANCE · MEXICO · CHILE · UNITED STATES · AUSTRALIA

TOTAL NUMBER OF YEARS OF MANDATORY SCHOOLING

8 · 9 · 9 · 9 · 9 · 9 · 9 · 8 · 9 · 9 · 9 · 9 · 8 · 9 · 11

2/ AGE AT WHICH CHILDREN START SCHOOL

12% **78%** **16%**

3-5 YEARS OLD · 6 YEARS OLD · 7 YEARS OLD

3/ AGE AT WHICH CHILDREN START SCHOOL

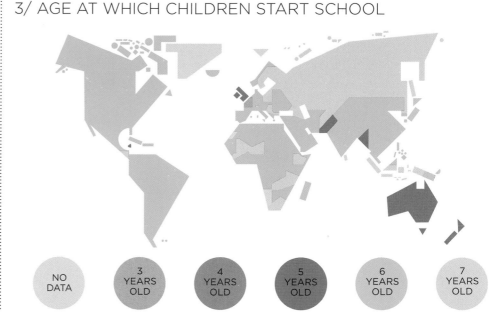

NO DATA · 3 YEARS OLD · 4 YEARS OLD · 5 YEARS OLD · 6 YEARS OLD · 7 YEARS OLD

4/ NUMBER OF CHILDREN AROUND THE WORLD WHO ARE NOT IN SCHOOL

BASED ON DATA RECOGNIZING ONLY TWO GENDER OPTIONS

BOYS

GIRLS

NUMBER OF PRIMARY SCHOOL-AGED CHILDREN WHO DO NOT GO TO SCHOOL (IN MILLIONS)

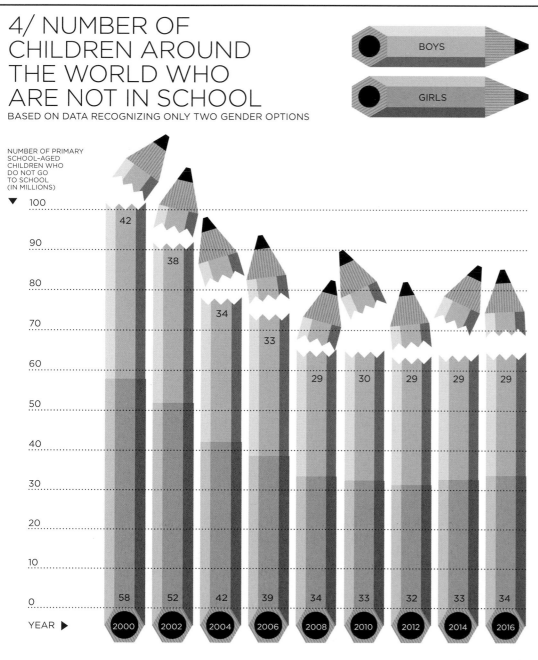

YEAR	2000	2002	2004	2006	2008	2010	2012	2014	2016
(top)	42	38	34	33	29	30	29	29	29
(bottom)	58	52	42	39	34	33	32	33	34

5/ WHAT ARE OLDER STUDENTS AROUND THE WORLD STUDYING?

BASED ON DATA COLLECTED FROM POSTSECONDARY STUDENTS

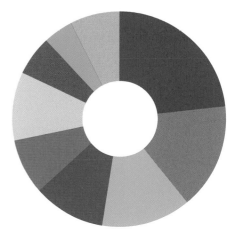

BUSINESS, ADMINISTRATION, AND LAW	**23%**
ENGINEERING, MANUFACTURING, AND CONSTRUCTION	**16%**
HEALTH AND WELFARE	13%
ARTS AND HUMANITIES	**11%**
SOCIAL SCIENCES, JOURNALISM, AND INFORMATION	**10%**
EDUCATION	9%
NATURAL SCIENCES, MATHEMATICS, AND STATISTICS	**6%**
INFORMATION AND COMMUNICATION TECHNOLOGIES	5%
OTHER FIELDS	7%

1/ Some school uniform styles from around the world

Countries shown: AUSTRALIA, CUBA, UNITED KINGDOM, SOUTH KOREA, NORTH KOREA, NIGERIA, SOUTH AFRICA, PERU, SRI LANKA

12. UNIFORMS

{
1/ Some school uniform styles from around the world

2/ Average number of students in a primary school classroom
}

2/ AVERAGE NUMBER OF STUDENTS IN A PRIMARY SCHOOL CLASSROOM

CHILE	CHINA	FRANCE	ICELAND	ITALY	JAPAN
30	37	23	19	19	27

IN SPAIN, MANY KIDS DO NOT WEAR UNIFORMS TO SCHOOL. WE DRESS COMFORTABLY, AND WE CAN USUALLY WEAR DIFFERENT OUTFITS. IN SOME OTHER COUNTRIES, KIDS WEAR UNIFORMS, AND SOMETIMES THEY EVEN HAVE A DIFFERENT UNIFORM DEPENDING ON THE TIME OF YEAR.

MEXICO	NETHERLANDS	POLAND	PORTUGAL	SPAIN	UNITED KINGDOM	UNITED STATES
22	23	19	21	22	26	21

This is my class ↗ (under SPAIN)

13. FOOD IN THE CAFETERIA

BY LUNCHTIME, WE ARE ALL HUNGRY! WE GO TO EAT IN THE CAFETERIA, WHERE EVERYONE LINES UP TO FILL THEIR TRAY WITH FOOD. IT WOULD BE FUN TO TRY ALL THE DIFFERENT LUNCHES THAT ARE SERVED IN COUNTRIES AROUND THE WORLD—LIKE ALL OF THESE!

Common foods eaten for school lunch in different countries

ITALY
Pasta, fish with arugula, tomato salad, fruit, and a muffin.

CZECH REPUBLIC
Potato and mushroom soup, *knedlíky* (bread dumplings), pork in a sauce, and pickled cabbage. A cup of apple juice.

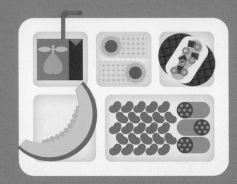

UNITED KINGDOM
Sausages and beans, corn on the cob, a slice of melon, a baked potato, and apple juice.

BRAZIL
Rice with black beans, baked plantain, pork and bell peppers, salad with tomatoes, and a seeded roll.

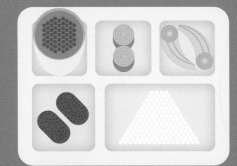

CUBA
Yellow pea soup, white rice, chicken croquettes, and a piece of taro root. A fried plantain for dessert.

CHINA
Hot soup with fresh vegetables, rice, steamed dumplings, noodles, and milk.

JAPAN
Miso soup, *takoyaki* (fried squid balls), salmon, white rice, and milk.

NORWAY
Open-faced sandwich of whole wheat bread with meat, cheese, and fish layers, with carrots and grapes or an apple. A glass of water or milk.

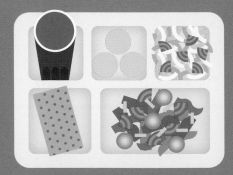

SWEDEN
Vegetable stew with boiled potatoes, coleslaw with carrots, and a cracker. A cup of lingonberry juice.

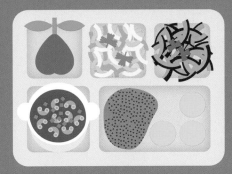

POLAND

Zupa pomidorowa (tomato soup) with pasta and parsley, a breaded pork chop with boiled potatoes, and *surówka* (a salad with fresh vegetables). For dessert, an apple, pear, or peach.

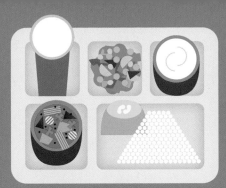

INDIA

Thali (a platter of various dishes) featuring white rice, *sambar* (lentil and tamarind soup), *dahi* (homemade yogurt or curd), sautéed vegetables with smoked pumpkin, and *rava kesari* (a sweet dessert made of semolina), and a cup of buttermilk.

UNITED STATES

Chicken nuggets with ketchup, mashed potatoes, peas, a fruit cup, and for dessert, a chocolate chip cookie.

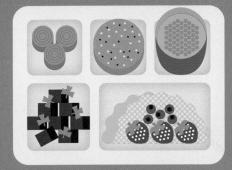

FINLAND

Pea soup, carrots, beet salad, a roll, and for dessert, a sweet crepe with berries.

SOUTH KOREA

Fish soup, broccoli, bell peppers, fried rice with tofu, and fermented cabbage.

FRANCE

Steak with green beans and carrots, a piece of Brie cheese, an apple, and a kiwi.

This is my food

SPAIN

Gazpacho (cold vegetable soup), paella (a rice dish with meat, seafood, and vegetables), tricolor bell pepper salad, and a roll. For dessert, an orange.

UKRAINE

Borscht (beet soup) with pickled cabbage, sausage, mashed potatoes, and a glass of water. For dessert, a sweet crepe.

TANZANIA

Chicken in sauce, cooked greens and vegetables, *ugali* (cornmeal porridge), and watermelon. A glass of water.

GREECE

Baked chicken with orzo, *dolmades* (stuffed grape leaves), cucumber and tomato salad, yogurt with pomegranate seeds, and two tangerines.

RUSSIA

Borscht (beet soup), veal chops, buckwheat, rye bread, and a cup of apple juice.

PORTUGAL

Chickpea soup, grilled sardines, boiled potatoes, salad with tomatoes, and an apple.

14. HOMEWORK

I LEAVE SCHOOL WITH MY BACKPACK ALL FILLED UP, AND THE FIRST THING I DO ONCE I GET HOME IS HAVE AN AFTER-SCHOOL SNACK. AFTER I TAKE A BREAK, MY PARENTS ASK ME: "DO YOU HAVE HOMEWORK TODAY?" MY ANSWER IS USUALLY YES. THERE ARE KIDS IN MANY COUNTRIES WHO SPEND A LONG TIME ON THEIR HOMEWORK EVERY NIGHT. SOME OF THE ASSIGNMENTS CAN BE VERY STRESSFUL, BUT SOME ARE REALLY FUN!

1/ Number of hours spent on homework each week

2/ Number of hours per week parents spend helping with homework

1/ NUMBER OF HOURS SPENT ON HOMEWORK EACH WEEK

BASED ON DATA COLLECTED FROM 15-YEAR-OLD STUDENTS

HOURS PER WEEK ▼

9 — 8.7
8
7 — 6.6
6 — 6.5 · This is my homework · 6.1
5 — 5.1 · 4.9 · 4.7
4
3
2
1
0

ITALY · POLAND · SPAIN · UNITED STATES · FRANCE · UNITED KINGDOM · GERMANY

2/ NUMBER OF HOURS PER WEEK PARENTS SPEND HELPING WITH HOMEWORK

HOURGLASS REPRESENTS TOTALITY OF PARENT RESPONSES IN EACH COUNTRY
AVERAGES ROUNDED TO THE NEAREST WHOLE NUMBER

INDIA	TURKEY	BRAZIL	RUSSIA	CHINA	SOUTH AFRICA	POLAND
12 hours per week	9 hours per week	8 hours per week	8 hours per week	7 hours per week	7 hours per week	6 hours per week

>7 hours   2–7 hours
<2 hours   0 hours

UNITED STATES	GERMANY	SOUTH KOREA	SPAIN	AUSTRALIA	FRANCE	UNITED KINGDOM	JAPAN
6 hours per week	5 hours per week	5 hours per week	5 hours per week	4 hours per week	4 hours per week	4 hours per week	3 hours per week

3.8	3.8	3.5	3.1	2.9	2.8
JAPAN	PORTUGAL	CHILE	CZECH REPUBLIC	SOUTH KOREA	FINLAND

15. INTERNET
AND SOCIAL MEDIA

1/ DAILY TIME LIMITS ESTABLISHED BY PARENTS
BECAUSE OF ROUNDING, PERCENTS ADD UP TO SLIGHTLY LESS THAN 100%

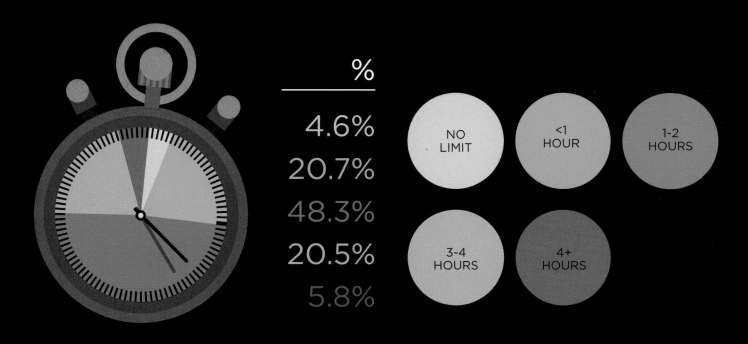

%
4.6%
20.7%
48.3%
20.5%
5.8%

NO LIMIT

<1 HOUR

1-2 HOURS

3-4 HOURS

4+ HOURS

2/ AVERAGE WEEKLY SCREEN TIME OF CHILDREN AROUND THE WORLD
BASED ON DATA FROM 29 COUNTRIES, WITH MULTIPLE ANSWERS POSSIBLE.
DOES NOT ACCOUNT FOR CHILDREN WHO DON'T HAVE A CELL PHONE BUT STILL ACTIVELY PARTICIPATE IN SOCIAL MEDIA

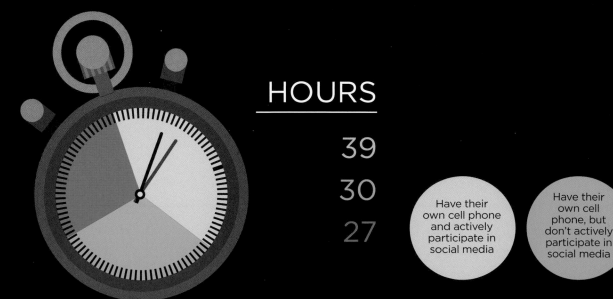

HOURS
39
30
27

Have their own cell phone and actively participate in social media

Have their own cell phone, but don't actively participate in social media

Don't have their own cell phone

I'VE FINALLY FINISHED MY HOMEWORK AND NOW I CAN RELAX. MY PARENTS LET ME SPEND SOME TIME ON THE INTERNET AND SOCIAL MEDIA, BUT TIME PASSES SO QUICKLY WHEN I'M IN FRONT OF THE SCREEN! MY MOM TELLS ME THAT I HAVE TO TURN MY DEVICES OFF AND GO TO BED.

1/ Daily time limits established by parents

2/ Average weekly screen time of children around the world

3/ Devices that children around the world use for internet access

3/ DEVICES THAT CHILDREN AROUND THE WORLD USE FOR INTERNET ACCESS
BASED ON DATA FROM 29 COUNTRIES, WITH MULTIPLE ANSWERS POSSIBLE

22% FAMILY TABLET

4% INTERNET CAFE

31% PERSONAL TABLET

49% PERSONAL CELL PHONE

38% FAMILY COMPUTER

29% SCHOOL COMPUTER

7% OTHER PUBLIC FACILITIES

26% FAMILY CELL PHONE

26% PERSONAL COMPUTER

16. READING

I MAKE TIME TO READ BEFORE I GO TO SLEEP AND ESPECIALLY DURING THE WEEKEND. AT SCHOOL, WE ARE REQUIRED TO READ BOOKS FOR OUR CURRICULUM, BUT AT HOME I LIKE TO READ DIFFERENT BOOKS. SOME COUNTRIES HAVE MORE PEOPLE WHO BUY BOOKS REGULARLY THAN OTHERS.

1/ The 10 bestselling books in the world

2/ Required reading in schools around the world

3/ Hours the average person spends reading per week

1/ THE 10 BESTSELLING BOOKS IN THE WORLD
EXCLUDING RELIGIOUS OR POLITICAL TEXTS

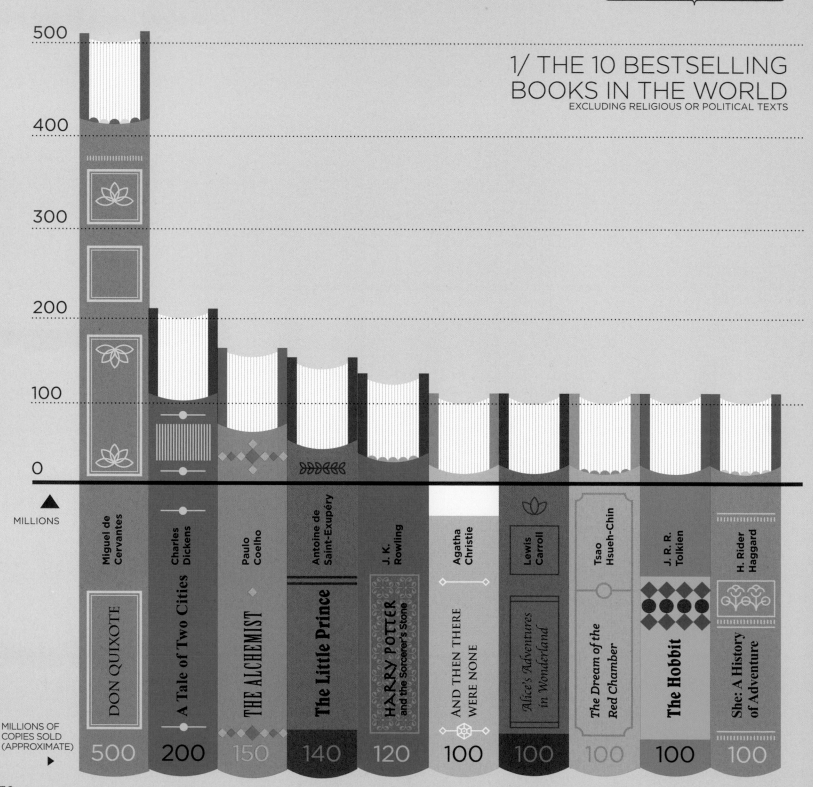

▲ MILLIONS

MILLIONS OF COPIES SOLD (APPROXIMATE) ►

Author	Title	Millions
Miguel de Cervantes	DON QUIXOTE	500
Charles Dickens	A Tale of Two Cities	200
Paulo Coelho	THE ALCHEMIST	150
Antoine de Saint-Exupéry	The Little Prince	140
J. K. Rowling	HARRY POTTER and the Sorcerer's Stone	120
Agatha Christie	AND THEN THERE WERE NONE	100
Lewis Carroll	Alice's Adventures in Wonderland	100
Tsao Hsueh-Chin	The Dream of the Red Chamber	100
J. R. R. Tolkien	The Hobbit	100
H. Rider Haggard	She: A History of Adventure	100

2/ REQUIRED READING IN SCHOOLS AROUND THE WORLD

Title	Author	Country
Chronicle in Stone	Ismail Kadare	ALBANIA
Tomorrow, When the War Began	John Marsden	AUSTRALIA
Faust	Johann Wolfgang von Goethe	AUSTRIA
The Bridge on the Drina	Ivo Andrić	BOSNIA SERBIA
The Death and Life of Severino	João Cabral de Melo Neto	BRAZIL
The Wars	Timothy Findley	CANADA
Sub Terra	Baldomero Lillo	CHILE
The Analects	Confucius	CHINA
One Hundred Years of Solitude	Gabriel García Márquez	COLOMBIA
The Days	Taha Hussein	EGYPT
Seven Brothers	Aleksis Kivi	FINLAND
The Diary of Anne Frank	Anne Frank	GERMANY
Things Fall Apart	Chinua Achebe	GHANA NIGERIA
Autobiography: The Story of My Experiments with Truth	Mohandas K. Gandhi	INDIA
The Betrothed	Alessandro Manzoni	ITALY
The Reluctant Fundamentalist	Mohsin Hamid	PAKISTAN
War and Peace	Leo Tolstoy	RUSSIA
Touch Me Not	José Rizal	PHILIPPINES
To Kill a Mockingbird	Harper Lee	UNITED STATES
The Tale of Kiều	Nguyễn Du	VIETNAM

3/ HOURS THE AVERAGE PERSON SPENDS READING PER WEEK

COUNTRY ▼	TIME PER WEEK ▼
INDIA	10 HOURS, 42 MINUTES
THAILAND	9 HOURS, 24 MINUTES
CHINA	8 HOURS, 00 MINUTES
PHILIPPINES	7 HOURS, 36 MINUTES
EGYPT	7 HOURS, 30 MINUTES
CZECH REPUBLIC	7 HOURS, 24 MINUTES
RUSSIA	7 HOURS, 06 MINUTES
SWEDEN	6 HOURS, 54 MINUTES
FRANCE	6 HOURS, 54 MINUTES
HUNGARY	6 HOURS, 48 MINUTES
SAUDI ARABIA	6 HOURS, 48 MINUTES
HONG KONG	6 HOURS, 42 MINUTES
POLAND	6 HOURS, 30 MINUTES
VENEZUELA	6 HOURS, 24 MINUTES
SOUTH AFRICA	6 HOURS, 18 MINUTES
AUSTRALIA	6 HOURS, 18 MINUTES
INDONESIA	6 HOURS, 00 MINUTES
ARGENTINA	5 HOURS, 54 MINUTES
TURKEY	5 HOURS, 54 MINUTES
SPAIN	5 HOURS, 48 MINUTES
CANADA	5 HOURS, 48 MINUTES
GERMANY	5 HOURS, 42 MINUTES
UNITED STATES	5 HOURS, 42 MINUTES
ITALY	5 HOURS, 36 MINUTES
MEXICO	5 HOURS, 30 MINUTES
UNITED KINGDOM	5 HOURS, 18 MINUTES
BRAZIL	5 HOURS, 12 MINUTES
TAIWAN	5 HOURS, 00 MINUTES
JAPAN	4 HOURS, 06 MINUTES
KOREA	3 HOURS, 06 MINUTES

For comparison, the average number of hours a person spends per week watching television (based on a study of 94 countries):

Watching TV	20 hours, 42 minutes

17. SPORTS
AROUND THE WORLD

1/ Most popular spectator sports in each country

2/ Most commonly played sports in the world

1/ MOST POPULAR SPECTATOR SPORTS IN EACH COUNTRY

SOCCER

ICE HOCKEY

AMERICAN FOOTBALL

BASEBALL

CRICKET

BOXING

AT SCHOOL AND ON THE WEEKENDS, I PLAY SPORTS! I LIKE SWIMMING THE BEST. EVERY COUNTRY HAS ITS MOST POPULAR SPORTS. IN SPAIN AND IN MANY OTHER COUNTRIES, ONE OF THE MOST POPULAR SPORTS IS SOCCER. IT'S DEFINITELY THE ONE THAT PEOPLE IN MANY COUNTRIES WATCH THE MOST!

BASKETBALL

AUSTRALIAN FOOTBALL

RUGBY

GAELIC FOOTBALL

VOLLEYBALL

2/MOST COMMONLY PLAYED SPORTS IN THE WORLD
MILLIONS OF PLAYERS

This is my favorite!

SWIMMING
1500

SOCCER
1002

VOLLEYBALL
998

BASKETBALL
400

TENNIS
300

BADMINTON
200

BASEBALL
60

HANDBALL
18

HOCKEY
3

RUGBY
2

18. PLAYGROUND GAMES AROUND THE WORLD

Dinifri
MOROCCO

Two teams of five players stand in opposite corners of a square. They take turns throwing a stick and trying to knock down the column of stones in the center.

Kabaddi
BANGLADESH AND INDIA

Two teams of seven players each stand on opposite sides of a field. Each team sends one person (the "raider") to the opposite side. In order to earn a point, the raider must tag as many opposing players as possible, then return to their team's side of the field without being captured. The opposing team's defenders try to surround and capture the raider, who has to enter their side of the field singing "*kabaddi, kabaddi, kabaddi*" in a single breath. If the opposing team captures the raider, they get a point instead.

Tag
UNITED KINGDOM

In this game, everyone has to flee from the person who is it. The person who is it tries to tag someone else, at which point the person they have tagged either becomes the new it or is out of the game. In the second case, the game ends when the person who is it has successfully tagged everyone.

Ten Ten
NIGERIA

This is a game of hands and rhythm. Two players stand face-to-face, clapping and moving their legs in rhythm. They must make sure not to lift up the incorrect leg, because if they make a mistake their opponent will get a point.

I play this!

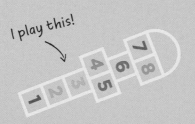

La Rayuela (Hopscotch)
SPAIN

In this game, a series of squares is drawn on the ground in white chalk. Players compete to see who can finish it fastest—by jumping in each square on just one leg. Each player takes a stone and throws it into one of the squares, then picks it up as they pass through that square, staying balanced on one leg the entire time.

La Víbora de la Mar (The Sea Snake)
MEXICO

Two players stand opposite each other, forming an arch with their raised arms. The rest of the players form a line and run under the arch like one long snake. All the players sing the Sea Snake song as the "snake" passes under the arch, and at the last line of each stanza, the players forming the arch bring their arms down to capture one of the players underneath.

Cache-Cache (Hide-and-Seek)
FRANCE

This is a very popular game. One player closes their eyes and counts up to 100, while all the other players hide. The player who was counting then opens their eyes and tries to find everyone who is hiding. The first person to be found becomes the next one to search, and the last person to be found is the winner.

Corre, Corre, la Guaraca (Run, Run, la Guaraca)
CHILE

In this game, players sit in a circle while a runner jogs around the edge of the circle with a handkerchief. The players in the circle cannot look at the runner, but they sing "run, run, *la guaraca*" (slingshot) as the runner circles. As gently as possible, the runner drops the handkerchief on the back of one of the players and then runs. If the runner makes it around the circle before the player realizes the handkerchief is on their back, that player is out. If the player does realize, they jump up and chase the runner. If the runner is tagged, they are out. If the runner makes it around the circle without being tagged, the player chasing them becomes the new runner.

Pilolo
GHANA

One player is chosen to hide sticks or stones secretly, while the other players are not looking. When the chosen player is done hiding the objects, he or she cries "*pilolo*!" ("time to search!") and starts timing the players, who begin searching for the objects. The players may sing a song while they are searching. When a player finds a stick, they run to touch the leader and get a point. The player with the most points wins!

Catch the Dragon's Tail
CHINA

Players stand in line and form a chain, holding hands or placing their arms on the shoulders of the player in front of them. The dragon's "head" (the player at the front of the chain) then tries to catch the dragon's "tail" (the player at the end of the chain), taking the entire chain along with her. All the players in the middle do their best to keep the tail from being caught, without ever breaking the chain.

DURING THE WEEKEND, I LIKE TO PLAY WITH MY FRIENDS IN THE PARK. THERE ARE SOME PLAYGROUND GAMES THAT HAVE EXISTED FOR MANY YEARS—OUR PARENTS MIGHT EVEN HAVE PLAYED THEM—AND OTHERS THAT HAVE ONLY RECENTLY BEEN INVENTED. EVERY COUNTRY HAS ITS OWN MOST POPULAR GAMES, AND MANY OF THESE GAMES ARE PLAYED IN MULTIPLE COUNTRIES AROUND THE WORLD! OFTEN THEY ARE ALMOST THE SAME BUT DIFFER IN HOW THEY ARE PLAYED OR WHAT THEY ARE CALLED.

Dodgeball
UNITED STATES

There are different versions of this game, but the teams usually have six players each and three balls available to each team. The goal of the game is to eliminate all the other team's players by hitting them below the shoulders with a ball.

Kho Kho
INDIA AND PAKISTAN

This game is played in two teams of 12 people. Eight players from one team enter the field and sit on their knees, facing in alternating directions, while the ninth player (the "chaser") stands at one end of the field. Three players from the other team (the "defenders") then enter the field and attempt to escape being tagged by the chaser for seven minutes, during which the chaser can tag any player who is sitting on their knees as a replacement.

Shadows
IRELAND

In this game, players try to step on their opponent's shadow. If a player successfully steps on a shadow, their opponent then attempts to chase and catch theirs. Players can run to a place in the shade, where their shadows can't be seen, in order to become safe.

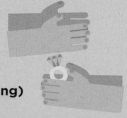

Podchody (Paper Chase)
POLAND

This is a fun game to play outside—especially in the woods. There are two teams of players. One team sets off first, leaving tracks and clues in the form of pieces of paper, arrows with sticks, letters, or other signs. After 15 minutes, the second group sets off after the first and attempts to find and catch the first team, following the trail of clues. If the first team makes it to the finish point without being caught, they win, but if the second team catches them, then that team wins.

Kolechko (Ring-Ring)
RUSSIA

Players sit in a row, each with their hands clasped together. One player, the leader, has a ring in their hands. This player walks down the row, clasping their hands around each of the other players' hands and passing one of them the ring in secret. The leader then says, "Ring-Ring, go out to the porch!" and the player who has the ring jumps up and tries to run away while the other players attempt to catch them. If they successfully evade being caught, they are the new leader.

Te-tsunagi Oni (Holding-Hands Tag)
JAPAN

One player chases all the others. When he or she catches somebody, they join hands and continue chasing the others. When the chain of players doing the chasing becomes very long, it can be split into two smaller chains. The game ends when all the players have been caught, making up one very long line.

Topfschlagen (Hit the Pot)
GERMANY

One of the players is chosen to stand blindfolded in the middle of the room. He or she is given a wooden spoon, then spun around. Somewhere in the room, a pot is placed upside down, covering a prize of chocolate or candy. The blindfolded player must crawl around the room using the wooden spoon to find the pot. If it's found, the player gets to eat the chocolate!

Statues
GREECE

One of the players stands blindfolded in the center of a field and starts to count. While he or she is counting, the other players run around the field. The player who is counting suddenly shouts "agalmata!" ("statues!"). At that moment, all the other players freeze, imitating statues, and the player in the center of the field removes the blindfold. If he or she catches anyone moving, they're out. It's hard not to laugh!

Piovra (Octopus)
ITALY

One player is chosen to be the octopus. The octopus stands absolutely still, and the other players stand about 20 steps away. All at once, all the players run toward the octopus—but they must try not to get captured! The octopus tries to capture other players, but he or she can only move sideways. Once the octopus tags another player, that player becomes a "baby octopus." The baby octopus is frozen in place, but can swing their arms around to try to help the octopus catch other players. When all the players have been captured, the first player to become a baby octopus is the new octopus.

19. SUMMER VACATIONS

FINALLY, SUMMER VACATION IS HERE! IN SPAIN, OUR SUMMER VACATION IS VERY LONG: 11 WHOLE WEEKS! BUT IN OTHER COUNTRIES, KIDS HAVE MORE DAYS OFF OVER THE COURSE OF THE ENTIRE SCHOOL YEAR. IN AUGUST, WHEN MY PARENTS ARE ALSO ON VACATION, WE TRY TO TRAVEL TO OTHER PLACES TOGETHER. MY GRANDPARENTS TELL ME THAT WHEN THEY WERE YOUNG, PEOPLE DID NOT TRAVEL AS MUCH AS THEY DO NOW.

1/ Weeks of summer vacation

2/ Growth in international tourism

3/ Countries visited by the most international tourists

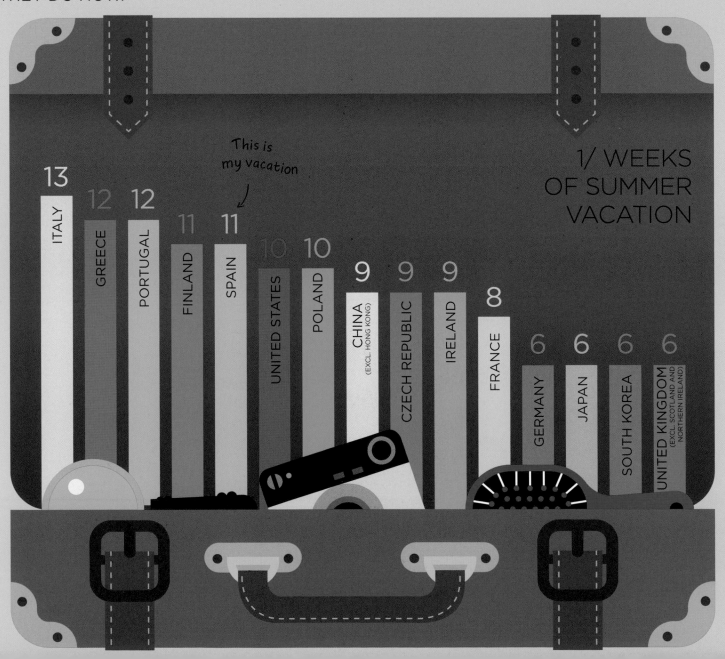

This is my vacation

1/ WEEKS OF SUMMER VACATION

- 13 ITALY
- 12 GREECE
- 12 PORTUGAL
- 11 FINLAND
- 11 SPAIN
- 10 UNITED STATES
- 10 POLAND
- 9 CHINA (EXCL. HONG KONG)
- 9 CZECH REPUBLIC
- 9 IRELAND
- 8 FRANCE
- 6 GERMANY
- 6 JAPAN
- 6 SOUTH KOREA
- 6 UNITED KINGDOM (EXCL. SCOTLAND AND NORTHERN IRELAND)

2/ GROWTH IN INTERNATIONAL TOURISM

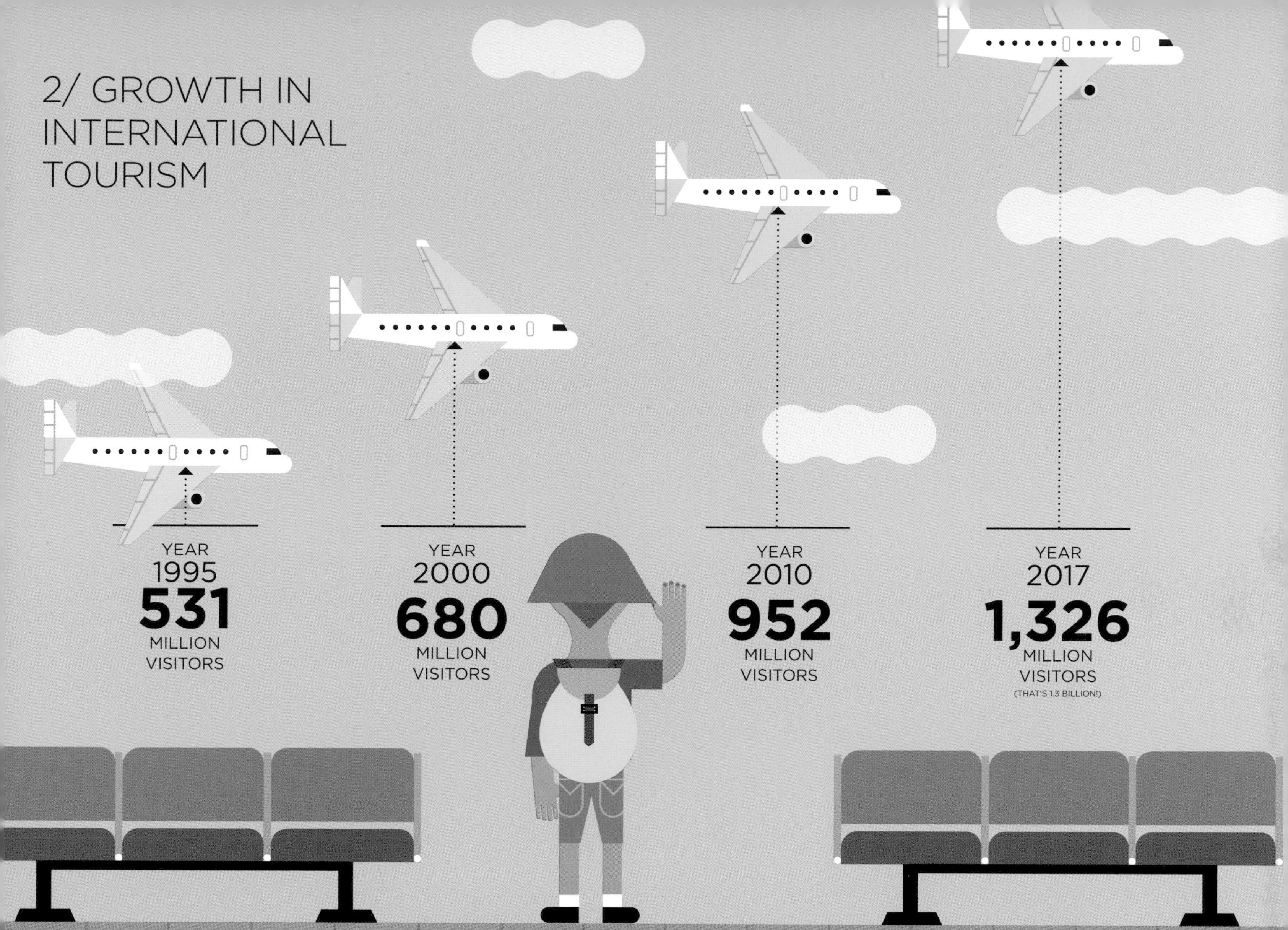

YEAR
1995
531
MILLION
VISITORS

YEAR
2000
680
MILLION
VISITORS

YEAR
2010
952
MILLION
VISITORS

YEAR
2017
1,326
MILLION
VISITORS
(THAT'S 1.3 BILLION!)

3/ COUNTRIES VISITED BY THE MOST INTERNATIONAL TOURISTS

BASED ON DATA COLLECTED IN 2017

EUROPE   NORTH AMERICA   ASIA

THAILAND
35.4
million

GERMANY
37.5
million

TURKEY
37.6
million

UNITED KINGDOM
37.7
million

MEXICO
39.3
million

ITALY
58.3
million

FRANCE
86.9
million

SPAIN
81.8
million

UNITED STATES
76.9
million

CHINA
60.7
million

20. MOST VISITED CITIES

1/ Most visited cities in the world

2/ Most visited museums in the world

1/ MOST VISITED CITIES IN THE WORLD

EUROPE   AFRICA   ASIA   OCEANIA   NORTH AMERICA   SOUTH AMERICA

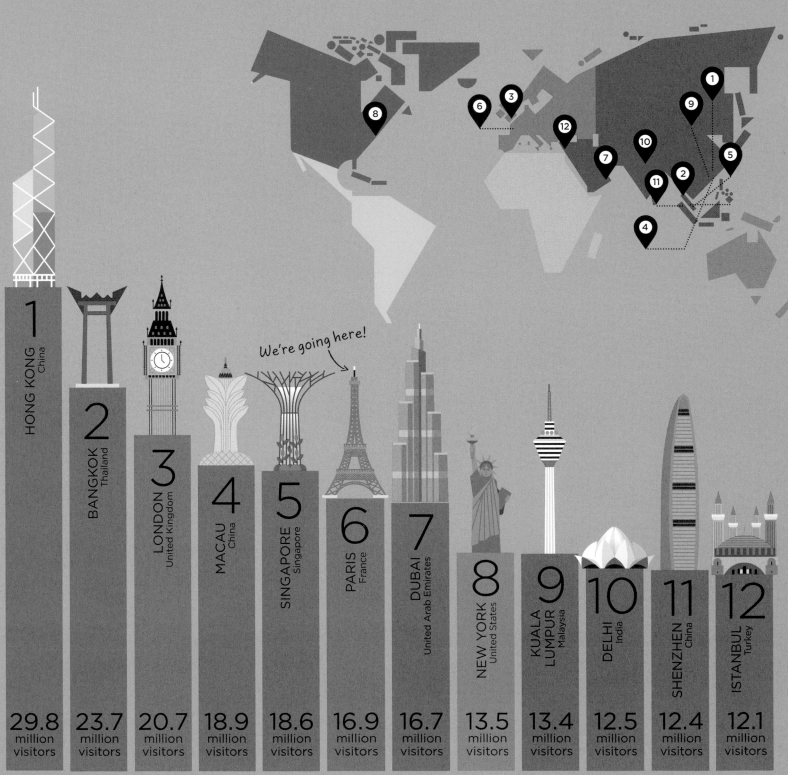

We're going here!

1	2	3	4	5	6	7	8	9	10	11	12
HONG KONG China	BANGKOK Thailand	LONDON United Kingdom	MACAU China	SINGAPORE Singapore	PARIS France	DUBAI United Arab Emirates	NEW YORK United States	KUALA LUMPUR Malaysia	DELHI India	SHENZHEN China	ISTANBUL Turkey
29.8 million visitors	23.7 million visitors	20.7 million visitors	18.9 million visitors	18.6 million visitors	16.9 million visitors	16.7 million visitors	13.5 million visitors	13.4 million visitors	12.5 million visitors	12.4 million visitors	12.1 million visitors

IN MY HOUSE, WE'VE BEEN TALKING ABOUT WHERE WE WANT TO GO ON VACATION. MY BROTHER WANTS TO VISIT THE GREAT PYRAMID OF GIZA IN CAIRO. MY MOTHER AND I WANT TO GO TO PARIS, AND MY FATHER CAN'T DECIDE. IN THE END, MY BROTHER COMPROMISED: WE WILL GO TO PARIS AND VISIT THE LOUVRE MUSEUM, WHERE HE CAN SEE THE COLOSSAL STATUE OF RAMESSES II INSTEAD. DID YOU KNOW THAT PARIS IS ONE OF THE MOST VISITED CITIES IN THE WORLD, AND THAT THE LOUVRE IS THE MOST VISITED MUSEUM IN THE WORLD?

2/ MOST VISITED MUSEUMS IN THE WORLD

1 million visitors

1 LOUVRE MUSEUM
Paris, France

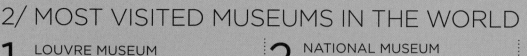

10.2

2 NATIONAL MUSEUM OF CHINA
Beijing, China

8.6

3 THE METROPOLITAN MUSEUM OF ART
New York, United States

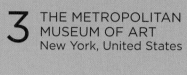

7.4

4 VATICAN MUSEUMS
Vatican City (Rome), Italy

6.8

5 NATIONAL AIR AND SPACE MUSEUM
Washington, DC, United States

6.2

6 BRITISH MUSEUM
London, United Kingdom

5.9

7 TATE MODERN
London, United Kingdom

5.8

8 NATIONAL GALLERY
London, United Kingdom

5.7

9 NATURAL HISTORY MUSEUM
London, United Kingdom

5.3

10 AMERICAN MUSEUM OF NATURAL HISTORY
New York, United States

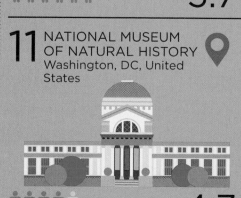

5

11 NATIONAL MUSEUM OF NATURAL HISTORY
Washington, DC, United States

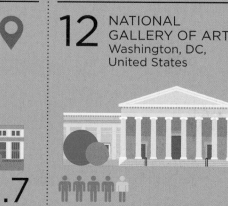

4.7

12 NATIONAL GALLERY OF ART
Washington, DC, United States

4.4

21. SOME WORDS TO USE WHILE TRAVELING

1/ Ways to say hello and thank you

2/ Ways to communicate with your hands

1/ WAYS TO SAY HELLO AND THANK YOU

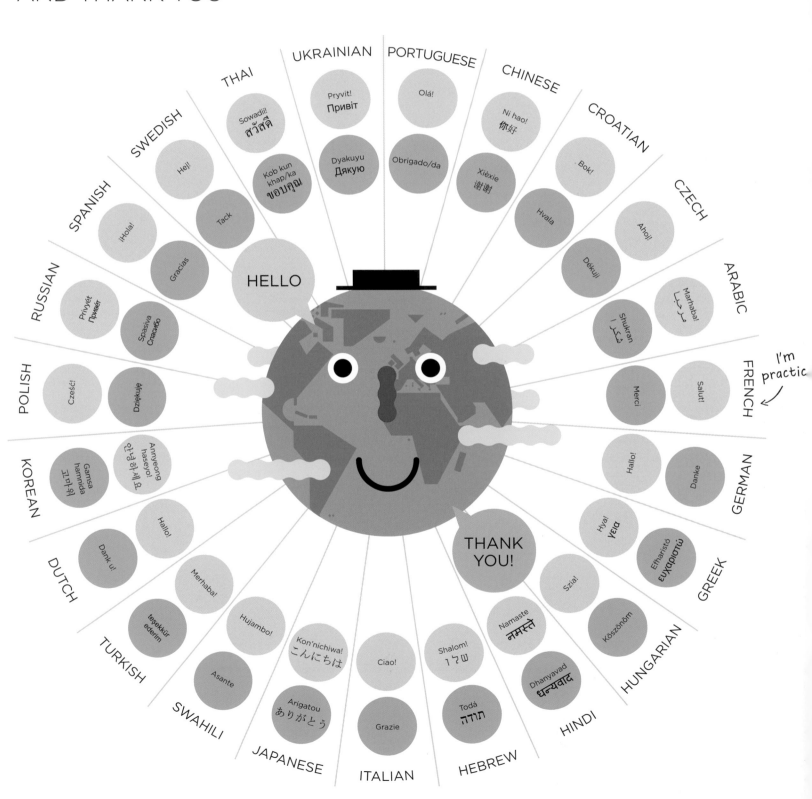

UKRAINIAN · PORTUGUESE · CHINESE · THAI · CROATIAN · SWEDISH · CZECH · SPANISH · ARABIC · RUSSIAN · FRENCH · POLISH · GERMAN · KOREAN · GREEK · DUTCH · HUNGARIAN · TURKISH · HINDI · SWAHILI · HEBREW · JAPANESE · ITALIAN

HELLO

THANK YOU!

I'm practic

UKRAINIAN — Pryvit! Привіт / Dyakuyu Дякую
PORTUGUESE — Olá! / Obrigado/da
CHINESE — Ni hao! 你好 / Xièxie 谢谢
THAI — Sowadii! สวัสดี / Kob kun khap/ka ขอบคุณ
CROATIAN — Bok! / Hvala
SWEDISH — Hej! / Tack
CZECH — Ahoj! / Děkuji
SPANISH — ¡Hola! / Gracias
ARABIC — Marhaba! مرحبا / Shukran شكراً
RUSSIAN — Privyét Привет / Spasiva Спасибо
FRENCH — Salut! / Merci
POLISH — Cześć! / Dziękuję
GERMAN — Hallo! / Danke
KOREAN — Annyeong haseyo! 안녕하세요 / Gamsa hamnida 감사합니다
GREEK — Yia! Γεια / Efharistó ευχαριστώ
DUTCH — Hallo! / Dank u!
HUNGARIAN — Szia! / Köszönöm
TURKISH — Merhaba! / teşekkür ederim
HINDI — Namaste नमस्ते / Dhanyavad धन्यवाद
SWAHILI — Hujambo! / Asante
HEBREW — Shalom! שלום / Todá תודה
JAPANESE — Kon'nichiwa! こんにちは / Arigatou ありがとう
ITALIAN — Ciao! / Grazie

IN PARIS, PEOPLE SPEAK FRENCH, SO MY FAMILY THOUGHT IT WOULD BE GOOD TO LEARN SOME FRENCH WORDS FOR OUR TRIP. WE WANTED TO KNOW HOW TO SAY HELLO AND THANK YOU. WHEN TRAVELING, IT'S ALSO HELPFUL TO COMMUNICATE WITH YOUR HANDS!

2/ WAYS TO COMMUNICATE WITH YOUR HANDS

FRANCE

Lift two fingers toward your nose:
It's as easy as this

Touch under your eye with your index finger:
I don't believe you

Hold up hands with fingers pinched together:
Worry or *stress*

JAPAN

Touch your nose with your index finger:
I or *Me*

Hold up two fingers, facing outward:
I am happy and having a good time! (often used in photos instead of smiling)

Cross your arms in front of your body, with your palms sideways:
Not allowed

CHINA

Link your pinky fingers, knuckles facing outward:
We have an agreement, and we wish it well in the future

Put your hand over your heart:
I sincerely promise

Make a circle with your thumb and middle finger, rest your chin on it, and scratch your cheek with your index finger:
Shame on you!

BRAZIL

Tap your jaw with the back of your hand:
That's not true! or *That's gossip!*

Show the back of your hand, fingers up, and repeatedly close your thumb against your index finger:
It's full or *It's crowded*

Hit your fingers with those of your other hand, palms up, and alternate hands:
I don't care!

GHANA

Scratch the palm of your left hand:
Money

Flap your hand toward your stomach, palms down:
Come here

Tap your stomach with your right hand, then raise hand:
Satisfaction

RUSSIA

Flick your throat with your index finger:
Let's get something to drink!

Stretch your left hand behind your head and scratch your right ear:
This is getting too complicated . . .

Trace your thumb across your throat:
I've had enough or *I'm full*

UNITED STATES & UNITED KINGDOM

Make a circle with your thumb and index finger, keeping other fingers raised:
Sounds good or *Okay!*

Cross your fingers:
Good luck!

Fist bump with someone else:
Friendly greeting or celebration

MEXICO

Raise your hand with palm facing inward:
Thank you!

Bunch your fingers together, facing upward, and shake them:
A lot of something

Tap the palm of your hand with the opposite elbow:
Stingy

SPAIN

Rapidly open and close your hands in front of your body:
It's crowded in here!

Clench arms, then move up and down from your waist:
Lazy or *sluggish*

Move your index and middle fingers down your face from your eyes:
I have no money

ITALY

Touch your finger to your cheek and twist:
It's delicious!

Cup your hands together, waving up and down:
I can't believe what you're saying!

Swipe your palm, face down, outward from your chin:
I couldn't care less

22. CLIMATES OF THE EARTH

1/ Countries according to average annual rainfall

2/ Cities according to average hours of annual sun

3/ Cities with the most extreme climates in the world

1/ COUNTRIES ACCORDING TO AVERAGE ANNUAL RAINFALL
SELECTION FROM DATA OF OVER 200 COUNTRIES

COLOMBIA
127.6 in (3,240 mm)

SÃO TOMÉ AND PRÍNCIPE
126.0 in (3,200 mm)

PAPUA NEW GUINEA
123.7 in (3,142 mm)

COSTA RICA
115.2 in (2,926 mm)

MALAYSIA
113.2 in (2,875 mm)

BRAZIL
69.3 in (1,761 mm)

NEW ZEALAND
68.2 in (1,732 mm)

JAPAN
65.7 in (1,668 mm)

CHILE
59.9 in (1,522 mm)

UNITED KINGDOM
48 in (1,220 mm)

SLOVENIA
45.7 in (1,162 mm)

IRELAND
44 in (1,118 mm)

FRANCE
34.1 in (867 mm)

PORTUGAL
33.6 in (854 mm)

BELGIUM
33.3 in (847 mm)

ITALY
32.8 in (832 mm)

SLOVAKIA
32.4 in (824 mm)

THE NETHERLANDS
30.6 in (778 mm)

MEXICO
29.8 in (758 mm)

UNITED STATES
28.1 in (715 mm)

DENMARK
27.7 in (703 mm)

GERMANY
27.6 in (700 mm)

CZECH REPUBLIC
26.7 in (677 mm)

CHINA
25.4 in (645 mm)

SPAIN
25 in (636 mm)

POLAND
23.6 in (600 mm)

TURKEY
23.3 in (593 mm)

ARGENTINA
23.3 in (591 mm)

HUNGARY
23.2 in (589 mm)

UKRAINE
22.2 in (565 mm)

RUSSIA
18.1 in (460 mm)

ISRAEL
17.1 in (435 mm)

MONGOLIA
9.5 in (241 mm)

IRAN
9 in (228 mm)

TUNISIA
8.1 in (207 mm)

QATAR
2.9 in (74 mm)

SAUDI ARABIA
2.3 in (59 mm)

LIBYA
2.2 in (56 mm)

EGYPT
0.7 in (18 mm)

3/ CITIES WITH THE MOST EXTREME CLIMATES IN THE WORLD

The coldest city in the world
YAKUTSK
Russia

The temperature often drops below −40° Fahrenheit (−40° Celsius). The lowest temperature ever registered in this city is −84° Fahrenheit (−64.4° Celsius).

The hottest city in the world
KUWAIT CITY
Kuwait

The average annual temperature is 93.7° Fahrenheit (34.3° Celsius). In the summer, the highest temperatures average between 113–116.6° Fahrenheit (45–47° Celsius).

MY DAD SAYS THAT WHEN WE TO TRAVEL TO PARIS, WE NEED TO BRING RAINCOATS, SINCE IT RAINS MORE THAN WE'RE USED TO. BUT PARIS ISN'T THE RAINIEST PLACE IN THE WORLD! THERE ARE MANY WARM COUNTRIES IN THE WORLD, ESPECIALLY IN THE TROPICS, WHERE IT *REALLY* RAINS A LOT. THERE ARE CITIES THAT ENJOY MANY HOURS OF SUN, AND OTHERS IN WHICH THE CLIMATE CAN GET EXTREME: VERY COLD, VERY HOT, OR VERY WINDY.

2/ CITIES ACCORDING TO AVERAGE HOURS OF ANNUAL SUN

SELECTION FROM SUNSHINE AVERAGES FOR MORE THAN 120 COUNTRIES OVER A 30-YEAR PERIOD (1961–1990)

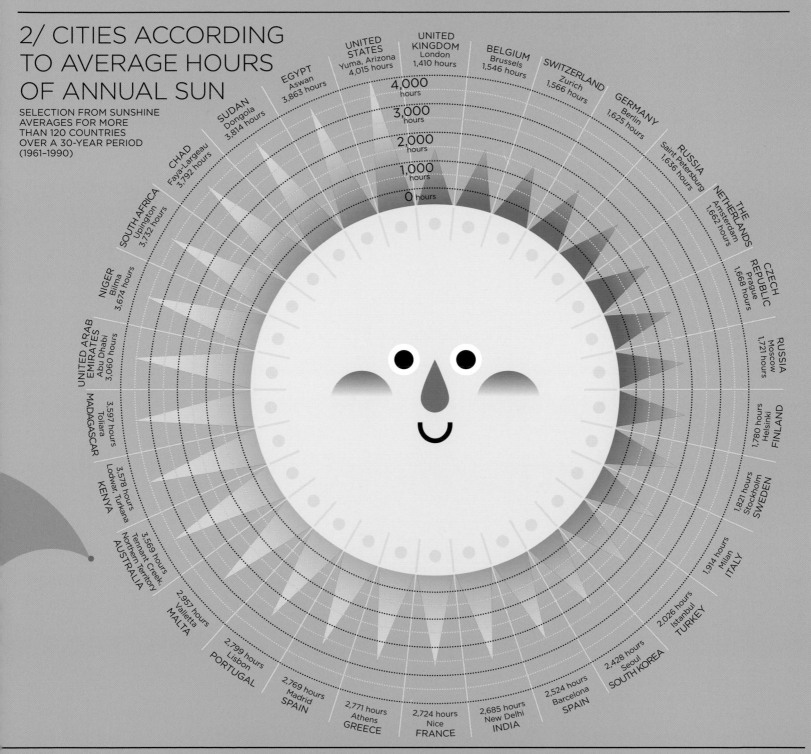

UNITED STATES Yuma, Arizona 4,015 hours
UNITED KINGDOM London 1,410 hours
BELGIUM Brussels 1,546 hours
SWITZERLAND Zurich 1,566 hours
EGYPT Aswan 3,863 hours
GERMANY Berlin 1,625 hours
SUDAN Dongola 3,814 hours
RUSSIA Saint Petersburg 1,636 hours
CHAD Faya-Largeau 3,792 hours
THE NETHERLANDS Amsterdam 1,662 hours
SOUTH AFRICA Upington 3,732 hours
CZECH REPUBLIC Prague 1,668 hours
NIGER Bilma 3,674 hours
RUSSIA Moscow 1,721 hours
UNITED ARAB EMIRATES Abu Dhabi 3,060 hours
FINLAND Helsinki 1,780 hours
MADAGASCAR Toliara 3,597 hours
SWEDEN Stockholm 1,821 hours
KENYA Lodwar, Turkana 3,578 hours
ITALY Milan 1,914 hours
AUSTRALIA Tennant Creek, Northern Territory 3,569 hours
TURKEY Istanbul 2,026 hours
MALTA Valletta 2,957 hours
SOUTH KOREA Seoul 2,428 hours
PORTUGAL Lisbon 2,799 hours
SPAIN Barcelona 2,524 hours
SPAIN Madrid 2,769 hours
INDIA New Delhi 2,685 hours
GREECE Athens 2,771 hours
FRANCE Nice 2,724 hours

4,000 hours
3,000 hours
2,000 hours
1,000 hours
0 hours

The driest city in the world
ASWAN
Egypt
Less than 0.04 inches (1 millimetre) of rain falls in this city every year. It almost never rains here, but there is a large source of water: the Nile River runs right through this city!

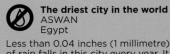
The wettest city in the world
BUENAVENTURA
Colombia
More than 247 inches (6,275 millimetres) of rain falls in this city every year.

The windiest city in the world
WELLINGTON
New Zealand
There are an average of 22 days per year where wind speeds are higher than 46 miles per hour (74 kilometres per hour), and 173 days per year where wind speeds are higher than 37 miles per hour (59 kilometres per hour).

23. BIRTHDAYS

MY BIRTHDAY IS SEPTEMBER 7, RIGHT BEFORE WE GO BACK TO SCHOOL AFTER SUMMER BREAK. ON THAT DAY, MY MOTHER MAKES MY FAVORITE FOODS AND I THROW A PARTY WITH MY FRIENDS. WE PLAY GAMES AND I BLOW OUT THE CANDLES ON THE CAKE. TODAY I AM 11 YEARS OLD! DID YOU KNOW THAT MOST PEOPLE AROUND THE WORLD CELEBRATE THEIR BIRTHDAYS IN SEPTEMBER?

1/ MONTHS OF THE YEAR WHEN MOST PEOPLE IN THE WORLD ARE BORN

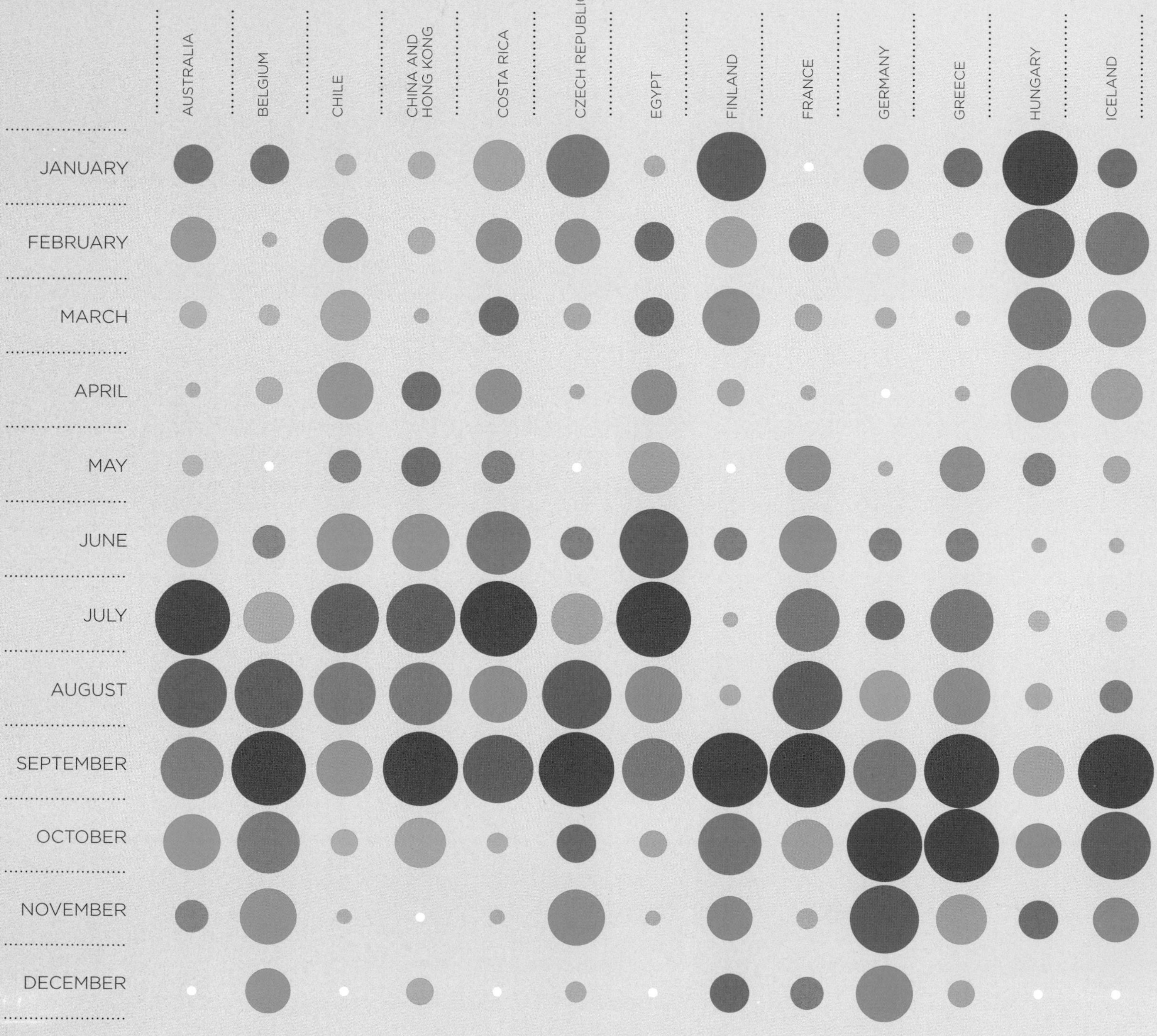

AUSTRALIA
BELGIUM
CHILE
CHINA AND HONG KONG
COSTA RICA
CZECH REPUBLIC
EGYPT
FINLAND
FRANCE
GERMANY
GREECE
HUNGARY
ICELAND
JANUARY
FEBRUARY
MARCH
APRIL
MAY
JUNE
JULY
AUGUST
SEPTEMBER
OCTOBER
NOVEMBER
DECEMBER

1/ Months of the year when most people in the world are born

2/ Things that happen between each of your birthdays

2/ THINGS THAT HAPPEN BETWEEN EACH OF YOUR BIRTHDAYS

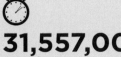

31,557,000 seconds have passed

Your heart has beat more than **42,000,000** times

The Earth has traveled more than **584** million miles (940 million kilometres) around the sun

 Your hair has grown almost **5** inches (12 centimetres) and your nails have grown **1.5** inches (4 centimetres)

 You have taken more than **10,500,000** breaths

HIGHEST NUMBER OF BIRTHS

LOWEST NUMBER OF BIRTHS

ISRAEL
ITALY
JAPAN
KOREA
MEXICO
NEW ZEALAND
RUSSIA
POLAND
PORTUGAL
SLOVENIA
SPAIN
SWITZERLAND
TURKEY
UKRAINE
UNITED STATES

I was born in this month

45

24. CHRISTMAS AROUND THE WORLD

CHRISTMAS IS COMING SOON! IT'S MY FAVORITE TIME OF THE YEAR. I LIKE THE CAROLS, GIFTS, SPECIAL MEALS, BEING WITH MY FAMILY, AND THE CAKES AND SWEETS WE EAT AT HOLIDAY PARTIES. CHRISTMAS ISN'T CELEBRATED EVERYWHERE IN THE WORLD, BUT IT *IS* AN IMPORTANT HOLIDAY IN MANY PLACES.

1/ HOW TO SAY "MERRY CHRISTMAS" IN 21 LANGUAGES

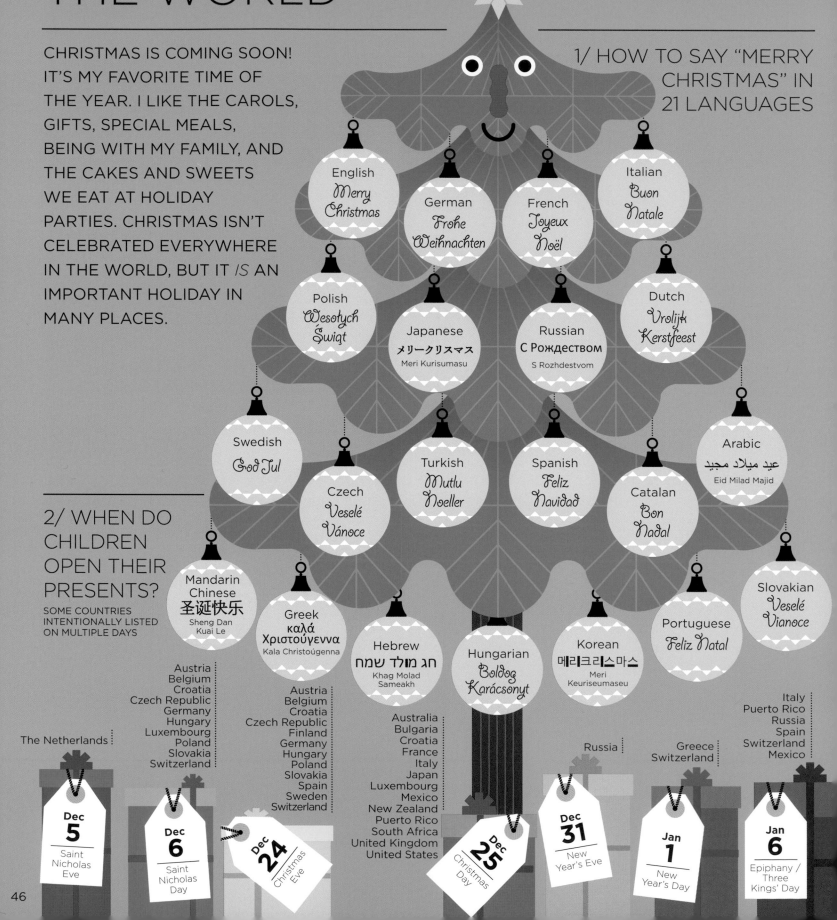

English
Merry Christmas

German
Frohe Weihnachten

French
Joyeux Noël

Italian
Buon Natale

Polish
Wesołych Świąt

Japanese
メリークリスマス
Meri Kurisumasu

Russian
С Рождеством
S Rozhdestvom

Dutch
Vrolijk Kerstfeest

Swedish
God Jul

Czech
Veselé Vánoce

Turkish
Mutlu Noeller

Spanish
Feliz Navidad

Catalan
Bon Nadal

Arabic
عيد ميلاد مجيد
Eid Milad Majid

Mandarin Chinese
圣诞快乐
Sheng Dan Kuai Le

Greek
καλά Χριστούγεννα
Kala Christoúgenna

Hebrew
חג מולד שמח
Khag Molad Sameakh

Hungarian
Boldog Karácsonyt

Korean
메리크리스마스
Meri Keuriseumaseu

Portuguese
Feliz Natal

Slovakian
Veselé Vianoce

2/ WHEN DO CHILDREN OPEN THEIR PRESENTS?

SOME COUNTRIES INTENTIONALLY LISTED ON MULTIPLE DAYS

Dec 5 — Saint Nicholas Eve
The Netherlands

Dec 6 — Saint Nicholas Day
Austria
Belgium
Croatia
Czech Republic
Germany
Hungary
Luxembourg
Poland
Slovakia
Switzerland

Dec 24 — Christmas Eve
Austria
Belgium
Croatia
Czech Republic
Finland
Germany
Hungary
Poland
Slovakia
Spain
Sweden
Switzerland

Dec 25 — Christmas Day
Australia
Bulgaria
Croatia
France
Italy
Japan
Luxembourg
Mexico
New Zealand
Puerto Rico
South Africa
United Kingdom
United States

Dec 31 — New Year's Eve
Russia

Jan 1 — New Year's Day
Greece
Switzerland

Jan 6 — Epiphany / Three Kings' Day
Italy
Puerto Rico
Russia
Spain
Switzerland
Mexico

3/ COUNTRIES IN WHICH CHRISTMAS IS A NATIONAL HOLIDAY

Christmas is not a national holiday

Christmas is a national holiday

4/ CHRISTMAS DESSERTS IN DIFFERENT COUNTRIES

Cougnou
BELGIUM

Bolo-rei
PORTUGAL

Bûche de Noël
FRANCE

Christmas cake
UNITED KINGDOM

Beigli
HUNGARY

Panettone
ITALY

Drømmekage
DENMARK

Japanese Christmas cake
JAPAN

Kersttulband
THE NETHERLANDS

Melomakarona
GREECE

Makowiec
POLAND

Vánočka
CZECH REPUBLIC

Perekladanets
UKRAINE

Štedrák
SLOVAKIA

Roscón de Reyes
SPAIN
MEXICO

This is for Three Kings' Day!

Stollen
GERMANY
AUSTRIA

Pan de Pascua
CHILE

47

25. RELIGIONS OF THE WORLD

1/ MAJORITY RELIGIONS IN DIFFERENT COUNTRIES

1/ Majority religions in different countries

2/ Major religions of the world

3/ Places of worship

4/ Foods that are allowed and prohibited in different religions

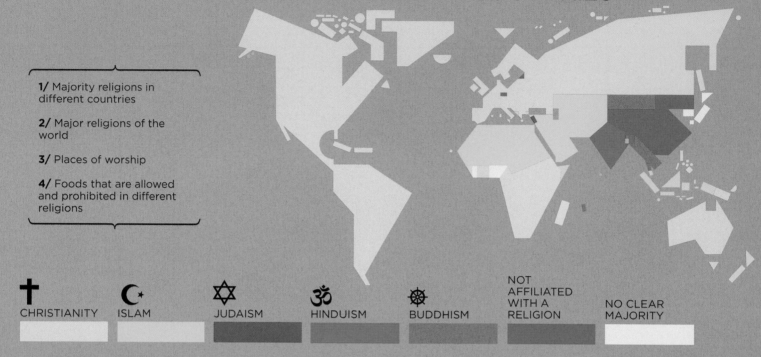

✝ CHRISTIANITY

☪ ISLAM

✡ JUDAISM

ॐ HINDUISM

☸ BUDDHISM

NOT AFFILIATED WITH A RELIGION

NO CLEAR MAJORITY

2/ MAJOR RELIGIONS OF THE WORLD

BY PERCENT OF THE POPULATION

%

31.1
24.9
15.6
15.2
6.6
5.6
0.8
0.2

BY NUMBER OF PEOPLE

Billions of people

2.38
1.94
1.91
1.16
0.51
0.43
0.06
0.01

CHRISTIAN   MUSLIM   UNAFFILIATED   HINDU   BUDDHIST   FOLK RELIGIONS   OTHER RELIGIONS   JEWISH

THERE ARE MANY RELIGIONS THROUGHOUT THE WORLD, AND PEOPLE BELIEVE IN DIFFERENT GODS AND DEITIES. WE ARE NOT VERY RELIGIOUS AT HOME, BUT OUR CULTURE IS FULL OF CUSTOMS AND FESTIVITIES RELATED TO RELIGION. THERE ARE LOTS OF BEAUTIFUL CHURCHES AND TEMPLES ALL OVER THE WORLD THAT I WOULD LIKE TO VISIT SOMEDAY.

3/ PLACES OF WORSHIP

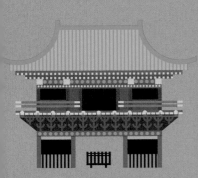

SHINTO SHRINE

Traditional Shinto ceremonies are performed outdoors. The gateway to the shrine, called the *torii*, is a symbol of Shintoism that marks the transition from the mundane to the sacred.

HINDU TEMPLE

These temples are also known as *mandir*. Most contain a great number of statues (called *murtis*) depicting the Hindu deity to which each temple is dedicated.

SYNAGOGUE

The synagogue is the gathering place of the Jewish faith, as well as a place of study and a place to worship God.

CATHEDRAL

These churches are also called "houses of God" by Catholics. Here the Catholic community meets to pray and participate in the ritual of Mass.

EASTERN ORTHODOX CHURCH

These churches, featuring traditional domes, are where Orthodox Christians hold their services and pray to God.

PROTESTANT CHURCH

This is where Protestants hold church services, worshipping God and Jesus.

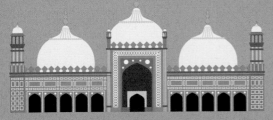

MOSQUE

Mosques are the place of worship for followers of the Islamic faith. This is where Muslims meet to pray to God, facing in the direction of Mecca.

BUDDHIST TEMPLE

This is the place of worship for Buddhists. There are different kinds of Buddhist temples and shrines, most commonly the pagoda, *stupa*, *wat*, and *chorten*.

4/ FOODS THAT ARE ALLOWED AND PROHIBITED IN DIFFERENT RELIGIONS

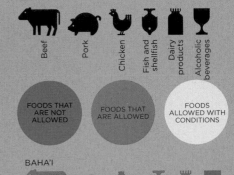

Beef | Pork | Chicken | Fish and shellfish | Dairy products | Alcoholic beverages

FOODS THAT ARE NOT ALLOWED

FOODS THAT ARE ALLOWED

FOODS ALLOWED WITH CONDITIONS

BAHA'I

BUDDHISM

Preferable to be a vegetarian and avoid eating any meat

PROTESTANT CHRISTIANITY

EASTERN ORTHODOX CHRISTIANITY

HINDUISM

ISLAM

Halal*   Halal*

ORTHODOX JUDAISM

Kosher** not with dairy   Kosher** not with dairy   No shellfish   Not with meat

MORMONISM

ROMAN CATHOLICISM

SIKHISM

Halal* and Kosher** in some sects

*HALAL refers to food that can be eaten in accordance with Islamic religious dietary law, which stipulates how the animal should be killed.

**KOSHER describes food and drink that complies with Jewish religious dietary law, which stipulates how the animal should be killed.

26.
IF THE WORLD ONLY HAD 100 PEOPLE

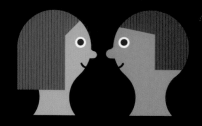

SOMETIMES, IT IS EASIER TO CONCEPTUALIZE THE WORLD IF WE IMAGINE THAT THERE ARE JUST A FEW PEOPLE IN IT. IF THERE WERE ONLY 100 PEOPLE IN THE WORLD, FOR INSTANCE . . .

DATA ASSUMES THAT EACH COLORFUL DOT IS ONE IMAGINED PERSON IN A WORLD WITH ONLY 100 PEOPLE

GENDER

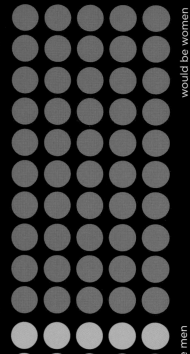

would be women

would be men

50 50

AGE

would be 0–14 years old

would be 15–24 years old

would be 25–64 years old

would be 65+ years old

25 16 50 9

GEOGRAPHY

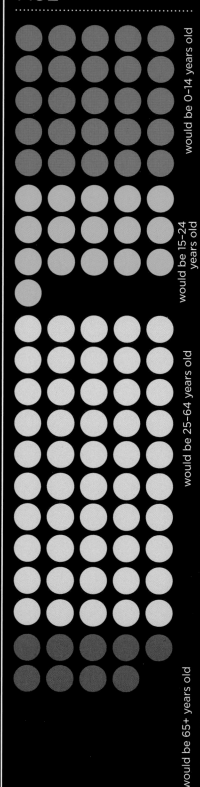

would live in Asia

would live in Africa

would live in Europe

would live in Latin America and the Caribbean

would live in North America

60 16 10 9 5

50

RELIGION

would be Christian

would be Muslim

would be unaffiliated with a religion

would be Hindu

would be Buddhist

would practice other religions (including Judaism)

31 24 16 15 7 7

FIRST LANGUAGE

flower

would speak Mandarin Chinese

would speak Spanish

would speak English

would speak Arabic

would speak Hindi

would speak Bengali

would speak Portuguese

would speak Russian

would speak Japanese

would speak Punjabi

would speak other languages

12 6 5 5 4 3 3 2 2 1 57

LITERACY

Based on data collected from people ages 15 and above

would be able to read and write

would not be able to read or write

86 14

URBAN/RURAL

would live in urban areas

would live in rural areas

55 45

SOURCES

1. COMMON NAMES

Most common names Mireia Trius, extensive research and firsthand evidence collected for *Yo y el Mundo,* Zahorí Books, 2019.

2. TYPES OF FAMILIES

1/ Average household size around the world "Average household size (most recent data since 2000)," Household Size and Composition Around the World 2017, United Nations, 2017, https://www .un.org/en/development/desa/population/ publications/pdf/ageing/household_ size_and_composition_around_the_ world_2017_data_booklet.pdf.

2/ Average number of children had by each woman "File FERT/4: Total fertility by region, subregion and country, 1950-2100 (live births per woman), Estimates, 1950 – 2020," World Population Prospects 2019, United Nations, Department of Economic and Social Affairs, Population Division, accessed online at https://population.un.org/ wpp/Download/Standard/Fertility/.

3/ Different family structures Based on Nathan Yau, "Most Common Family Types in America," Data Underload, FlowingData, July 20, 2016, https:// flowingdata.com/2016/07/20/modern-family-structure.

3. PETS

1/ Ten most popular dogs in the world "Most Popular Breeds Worldwide," DogWellNet.com, IPFD (International Partnership for Dogs), 2013, https://dogwellnet .com/content/population-statistics/ general-breeds-specific-disease-inform/information-on-breeding-animals/registries-health-information/ registration-figures-worldwide-%E2%80%93-from-top-thirty-to-endangered-breeds-r292/.

2/ Families with pets "Pet Ownership: Global GfK survey," Global Studies, GfK, May 2016, https:// www.gfk.com/fileadmin/user_ upload/country_one_pager/NL/ documents/Global-GfK-survey_Pet-Ownership_2016.pdf.

3/ Types of pets "Pet Ownership: Global GfK survey," Global Studies, GfK, May 2016, https://www.gfk.com/fileadmin/ user_upload/country_one_pager/NL/ documents/Global-GfK-survey_Pet-Ownership_2016.pdf.

4/ Most popular pets by country "Pet Ownership: Global GfK survey," Global Studies, GfK, May 2016, https://www.gfk .com/fileadmin/user_upload/country_ one_pager/NL/documents/Global-GfK-survey_Pet-Ownership_2016.pdf.

4. WORLD POPULATION

1/ Countries according to their number of inhabitants "Countries in the World by Population," Population, Worldometers, 2019, https://www .worldometers.info/world-population/ population-by-country/. Infographic inspired by Carrie Osgood, "Population of the World," *CarrieOnAdventures*, http://carrieonadventures.com/ inspiration/graphics/worldpopulation-detailed.png.

2/ Percentage of women and men in the world "Distribution of the World's Population by Age and Sex," World Population Prospects 2017, United Nations, Department of Economic and Social Affairs, Population Division, https://population.un.org/ wpp/Publications/Files/WPP2017_ DataBooklet.pdf.

3/ Projected population in future decades "Population of the world, SDG regions and selected groups of countries, 2019, 2030, 2050 and 2100, according to the medium-variant projection," World Population Prospects 2019, United Nations, Department of Economic and Social Affairs, Population Division, https://population.un.org/wpp/ Publications/Files/WPP2019_Highlights. pdf.

4/ Population distribution by region. "Population size, growth and age structure," World Population Prospects 2019, United Nations, Department of Economic and Social Affairs, Population Division, https://population.un.org/wpp/ Publications/Files/WPP2019_ Highlights.pdf.

5. LANGUAGES OF THE WORLD

1/ Most widely spoken languages in the world "Languages with at least 50 million first-language speakers," Ethnologue Global Dataset: Twenty-Second Edition Data, Ethnologue, 2019, https://www.ethnologue.com/statistics/ size.

2/ Map of the most widely spoken languages in the world "World Language Map," Maps of World, 2019, https://www.mapsofworld.com/world-language-map.htm.

3/ Languages most commonly studied as a second language "The World's Languages, in 7 Maps and Charts," by Rick Noack and Lazaro Gamino, *Washington Post,* 2015, https://www.washingtonpost.com/ news/worldviews/wp/2015/04/23/ the-worlds-languages-in-7-maps-and-charts/?noredirect=on&utm_term= .db031a267843, based on the data of Ulrich Ammon, University of Düsseldorf.

6. JOBS AND PROFESSIONS

1/ Some kinds of professions Mireia Trius, research and firsthand evidence collected for *Yo y el Mundo,* Zahorí Books, 2019.

2/ Five jobs that didn't exist before 2005 "10 Jobs That Didn't Exist 10 Years Ago," Rachel Hallett and Rosamund Hutt, World Economic Forum, 2016, https://www.weforum.org/ agenda/2016/06/10-jobs-that-didn-t-exist-10-years-ago/.

3/ What do the more than 7 billion people in the world do? Anna Vital, "What Do 7 Billion People Do," Funders and Founders, https://blog.adioma.com/ what-7-billion-world-population-does-infographic/, based on data from cia.gov, census.gov, and gemconsortium.org.

7. LIVING SPACES

1/ Average house size in different countries "How Big Is a House? Average New Home Size around the Globe in m², " Lindsay Wilson, Shrinkthatfootprint, 2013, http://shrinkthatfootprint.com/how-big-is-a-house, based on data from CommSec, RBA, UN, U.S. Census.

2/ Traditional houses from around the world Mireia Trius, research and firsthand evidence collected for *Yo y el Mundo,* Zahorí Books, 2019.

8. CITY POPULATIONS

1/ Select urban areas by number of inhabitants "Table 3: Built-Up Urban Areas by Land Area (Urban Footprint): 2019 Urban Areas 500,000 & Over Population," Demographia World Urban Areas, 15th Annual Edition, 2019, http://demographia.com/db-worldua.pdf.

2/ Select urban areas by population density "Table 4: Built-Up Urban Areas by Urban Population Density (Urban footprint): 2018 Urban Areas 500,000 & Over Population," Demographia World Urban Areas, 15th Annual Edition, 2019, http://demographia.com/db-worldua.pdf.

3/ Largest cities in 1950 "Table A.12. Population of urban agglomerations with 300,000 inhabitants or more in 2014," World Urbanization Prospects, 2014 Revision, United Nations, Department of Economic and Social Affairs, Population Division, https://population.un.org/wup/Publications/Files/WUP2014-Report.pdf. Infographic inspired by Joe Myers, "The world's 10 largest cities by 2030," World Economic Forum, 2016, https://www.weforum.org/agenda/2016/10/the-world-s-10-largest-cities-by-2030/.

4/ Largest cities predicted for 2030 "Population size and ranking of urban agglomerations with more than 5 million inhabitants as of 1 July 2018," World Urbanization Prospects, 2018 Revision, United Nations, Department of Economic and Social Affairs, Population Division, https://population.un.org/wup/Publications/Files/WUP2018-Highlights.pdf. Infographic inspired by Joe Myers, "The world's 10 largest cities by 2030," World Economic Forum, 2016, https://www.weforum.org/agenda/2016/10/the-world-s-10-largest-cities-by-2030/.

9. BREAKFAST FOODS AROUND THE WORLD

Children's breakfast rituals Mireia Trius, research and firsthand evidence collected for *Yo y el Mundo,* Zahorí Books, 2019.

10. TRAFFIC IN THE CITY

1/ Cities with the most traffic in the world "INRIX 2018 Global Traffic Scorecard," Global Traffic Scorecard, INRIX, 2018, http://inrix.com/scorecard/. Infographic inspired by Martin Armstrong, "The Cities with the Biggest Traffic Jams," Statista, 2019, https://www.statista.com/chart/12830/the-cities-with-the-biggest-traffic-jams/.

2/ Number of cars for every 10 people "World Vehicle Population Rose 4.6% in 2016," Wards Intelligence, WardsAuto, 2017, https://wardsintelligence.informa.com/WI058630/World-Vehicle-Population-Rose-46-in-2016.

11. AT SCHOOL

1/ Hours and years spent in mandatory schooling "Compulsory Instruction Time in General Education (2018) Primary and Lower Secondary Education, in Public Institutions," Education at a Glance 2018: OECD Indicators, 2018, OECD Publishing, https://read.oecd-ilibrary.org/education/education-at-a-glance-2018/compulsory-instruction-time-in-general-education-2018_eag-2018-graph173-en.

2-3/ Age at which children start school "Primary School Starting Age (Years)," UNESCO Institute for Statistics, World Bank, 2018, https://data.worldbank.org/indicator/SE.PRM.AGES?view=map. "Education," Welcome to France, Business France, 2019, https://www.welcometofrance.com/en/education.

4/ Number of children around the world who are not in school
"Out of School Population Among Children of Primary School Age (Millions) by Sex, 2000-2016," Institute for Statistics, UNESCO, 2018, https://data.unicef.org/topic/education/primary-education/.

5/ What are older students around the world studying? "What Do Young Adults Study?," Education at a Glance: OECD Indicators 2017, OECD Publishing, 2017, http://www.oecd.org/education/EAG2017-INFOGRAPHIC-ENGLISH.pdf.

12. UNIFORMS

1/ Some school uniforms styles from around the world Mireia Trius, research and firsthand evidence collected for *Yo y el Mundo,* Zahorí Books, 2019.

2/ Average number of students in a primary school classroom "Average Class Size by Type of Institution (2015) Average between Public and Private Schools," Education at a Glance, OECD Publishing, 2017, https://read.oecd-ilibrary.org/education/education-at-a-glance-2017/d2-1-average-class-size-by-type-of-institution-2015_eag-2017-table188-en.

13. FOOD IN THE CAFETERIA

Common food eaten for school lunch in different countries Mireia Trius, research and firsthand evidence collected for *Yo y el Mundo,* Zahorí Books, 2019. "School lunches around the world," Sweetgreen, 2015, https://sweetgreen.tumblr.com/post/103458679563/school-lunches-around-the-world.

14. HOMEWORK

1/ Number of hours spent on homework each week "Less homework, less stress?: Average time spent doing homework, 2003–2012," Trends Shaping Education 2016, OCED Publishing, 2016, https://read.oecd-ilibrary.org/education/trends-shaping-education-2016/less-homework-less-stress_trends_edu-2016-graph38-en.

2/ **Number of hours per week parents spend helping with homework** "Time Helping with Education," Global Parents' Survey 2018, The Varkey Foundation, 2018, https://www.varkeyfoundation.org/media/4340/vf-parents-survey-18-single-pages-for-flipbook.pdf.

15. INTERNET AND SOCIAL MEDIA

1/ **Daily time limits established by parents** "New Family Dynamics in a Connected World," Intel Security, 2017.

2/ **Average weekly screen time of children around the world** For children 8–12 years old. "2018 DQ Impact Report: Average Screen Time (Hours/Week)," DQ Institute, 2018, https://www.dqinstitute.org/2018dq_impact_report/.

3/ **Devices that children around the world use for internet access** For children 8–12 years old. "2018 DQ Impact Report: How 8-12 Year Olds Are Accessing the Internet (%)," DQ Institute, 2018, https://www.dqinstitute.org/2018dq_impact_report/.

16. READING

1/ **The 10 bestselling books in the world** "The World's Bestselling Novels," Mark Owuor Otieno, World Atlas, 2018, https://www.worldatlas.com/articles/best-selling-books.html. *Bibliophile: An Illustrated Miscellany*, Jane Mount, 2018. *The Nile: An Encyclopedia of Geography, History, and Culture*, John A. Shoup, 2017.

2/ **Required reading in schools around the world** "Required Reading: The Books That Students Read in 28 Countries around the World," TED, 2016, https://ideas.ted.com/required-reading-the-books-that-students-read-in-28-countries-around-the-world/.

3/ **Hours the average person spends reading per week** "Which Countries Read the Most? Hours Spent Reading per Person per Week (Selected Countries)," Statista, 2016, https://www.statista.com/chart/6125/which-countries-read-the-most/, based on data from NOP World CultureScore Index.

"One Television Year in the World," Eurodata TV, 2019, https://www.eurodatatv.com/en/one-television-year-world-0.

17. SPORTS AROUND THE WORLD

1/ **Most popular spectator sports in each country** "Soccer Unites the World," *National Geographic,* June 2006.

2/ **Most commonly played sports in the world** "The 10 Most Commonly Played Sports in the World," Sportzone, based on data from a survey of 204 Olympic committees.

18. PLAYGROUND GAMES AROUND THE WORLD

Common playground games around the world Mireia Trius, research and firsthand evidence collected for *Yo y el Mundo,* Zahorí Books, 2019.

19. SUMMER VACATIONS

1/ **Weeks of summer vacation** "The Organization of School Time in Europe, Primary and General Secondary Education 2018/2019," Eurydice, European Commission, 2018, https://eacea.ec.europa.eu/national-policies/eurydice/sites/eurydice/files/school_calendar_2018_19_final_report_0.pdf.

2/ **Growth in international tourism** "International Tourist Arrivals," UNWTO Tourism Highlights, World Tourism Organization, 2018, https://www.e-unwto.org/doi/pdf/10.18111/9789284419876.

3/ **Countries visited by the most international tourists** "World's Top Tourism Destinations," UNWTO Tourism Highlights, World Tourism Organization, 2018, https://www.e-unwto.org/doi/pdf/10.18111/9789284419876.

20. MOST VISITED CITIES

1/ **Most visited cities in the world** "Ranking and Notes," Top 100 City Destinations 2018, Euromonitor International, 2018, downloaded at https://go.euromonitor.com/white-paper-travel-2018-100-cities.html.

2/ **Most visited museums in the world** "Top 20 Museums Worldwide," Global Attractions Attendance Report, Themed Entertainment Association and AECOM, 2018, https://www.aecom.com/content/wp-content/uploads/2019/05/Theme-Index-2018-5-1.pdf.

21. SOME WORDS TO USE WHILE TRAVELING

1/ **Ways to say hello and thank you** "21 Ways to Say Hello," Living Language via SlideShare, 2014, https://www.slideshare.net/LivingLanguage/21-ways-to-say-hello. "23 Ways to Say Thank You," Living Language via SlideShare, 2014, https://www.slideshare.net/LivingLanguage/23-ways-to-say-thank-you.

2/ **Ways to communicate with your hands** "Around the World in 42 Hand Gestures," Worktheworld, 2016, https://www.worktheworld.com/infographics/around-world-42-hand-gestures, based on data from ISGS (International Society for Gesture Studies), *New York Post, Time*, CNN, No Worries Ghana, the *Guardian*, the Local (France), Zhiling and Guanhui's Nonverbal Communication, Speaking Latino. "80 British Gestures," Alex Case, UsingEnglish.com, 2019, https://www.usingenglish.com/articles/80-british-gestures.html.

22. CLIMATES OF THE EARTH

1/ **Countries according to average annual rainfall** "Aquastat," Food and Agriculture Organization of the United Nations, 2017, http://www.fao.org/nr/water/aquastat/data/query/results.html.

2/ **Cities according to average hours of annual sun** "Sunshine," UN Data, 2010, http://data.un.org/.

23. BIRTHDAYS

1/ Months of the year when the most people in the world were born "Which Birth Months Are Most Common Around the World?," Nayomi Chibana, Visme, 2017, https://visme.co/blog/most-common-birthday/, based on data from the United Nations Statistics Division.

2/ Things that happen between each of your birthdays Rayman, Mark. "Dear Dawniveraries," Dawn Journal (blog), Jet Propulsion Lab, California Institute of Technology, September 27, 2018, https://www.jpl.nasa.gov/blog/2018/9/dear-dawnniversaries. "Earth," NASA Science, Solar System Exploration, https://solarsystem.nasa.gov/planets/earth/in-depth/. Ostchega, et al., "National Health Statistics Report," Centers for Disease Control, August, 24, 2011, https://www.cdc.gov/nchs/data/nhsr/nhsr041.pdf. Susannah Fleming, et al., "Normal ranges of heart rate and respiratory rate in children from birth to 18 years," The Lancet, March 15, 2011, https://www.ncbi.nlm.nih.gov/pmc/articles/PMC3789232/.

24. CHRISTMAS AROUND THE WORLD

1/ How to say "Merry Christmas" in 21 languages "Merry Christmas in Different Languages," James Cooper, WhyChristmas?, https://www.whychristmas.com/customs/languages.shtml.

2/ When do children open their presents? "Christmas Around the World," James Cooper, WhyChristmas?, https://www.whychristmas.com/cultures/. The World Encyclopedia of Christmas, Gerry Bowler, 2000, accessed online via the Internet Archive.

3/ Countries in which Christmas is a national holiday "Countries That Recognize Christmas as a Public Holiday," Maphobbyist (Creative Commons), 2018, https://upload.wikimedia.org/wikipedia/commons/thumb/9/92/Countries_that_recognize_Christmas_as_a_Public_Holiday.png/800px-Countries_that_recognize_Christmas_as_a_Public_Holiday.png, based on data from "Holidays and Observances around the World,"
TimeandDate.com, https://www.timeanddate.com/holidays/.

4/ Christmas desserts in different countries "A Slice of Christmas: The Best Christmas Cakes from Around the World," Katarina Ferreira, Taxi2Airport, 2017, https://wp.taxi2airport.com/?p=2665.

25. RELIGIONS OF THE WORLD

1/ Majority religions in different countries "Majority Religion, By Country," The Global Religious Landscape, Pew Research Center, Pew-Templeton Global Religious Futures Project, 2012, https://assets.pewresearch.org/wp-content/uploads/sites/11/2014/01/global-religion-full.pdf.

2/ Major religions of the world "Worldwide All Population, 2020," Pew Research Center, Pew-Templeton Global Religious Futures Project, 2019, http://globalreligiousfutures.org/explorer#/?subtopic=15&chartType=bar&year=2010&data_type=number&religious_affiliation=all&destination=to&countries=Worldwide&age_group=all&gender=all.

3/ Places of worship. Mireia Trius, research and firsthand evidence collected for Yo y el Mundo, Zahorí Books, 2019.

4/ Foods that are allowed and prohibited in different religions. "Religious Dietary Restrictions," Fish Interfaith Center, Chapman University, https://www.chapman.edu/campus-life/fish-interfaith-center/_files/religious-dietary-restrictions.pdf.

26. IF THE WORLD ONLY HAD 100 PEOPLE

From 100 People: A World Portrait, compiled by Fritz J. Erickson and John A. Vonk, 2016, https://www.100people.org/statistics_detailed_statistics.php.

Gender. "People and Society: World: Sex Ratio," The World Factbook, Central Intelligence Agency, 2019, https://www.cia.gov/library/publications/the-world-factbook/geos/xx.html.

Age. "People and Society: World: Age Structure," The World Factbook, Central Intelligence Agency, 2019, https://www.cia.gov/library/publications/the-world-factbook/geos/xx.html.

Geography. "Distribution of the World's Population by Region, 2017," World Population Prospects 2017, United Nations, Department of Economic and Social Affairs, Population Division, https://population.un.org/wpp/Publications/Files/WPP2017_DataBooklet.pdf.

Religion. "Worldwide All Population, 2020," Pew Research Center, Pew-Templeton Global Religious Futures Project, 2019, http://globalreligiousfutures.org/explorer#/?subtopic=15&chartType=bar&year=2010&data_type=number&religious_affiliation=all&destination=to&countries=Worldwide&age_group=all&gender=all.

First language. "People and Society: World: Languages," The World Factbook, Central Intelligence Agency, 2019, https://www.cia.gov/library/publications/the-world-factbook/geos/xx.html.

Literacy. "People and Society: World: Literacy," The World Factbook, Central Intelligence Agency, 2019, https://www.cia.gov/library/publications/the-world-factbook/geos/xx.html.

Urban/Rural. "Urban Development," World Bank, 2018, https://data.worldbank.org/topic/urban-development.